Basic Training

Basic Training

PLAIN TALK ON THE KEY TRUTHS OF THE FAITH

R. C. Sproul

ZONDERVAN
PUBLISHING HOUSE
OF THE ZONDERVAN CORPORATION
GRAND RAPIDS, MICHIGAN 49506

BASIC TRAINING: PLAIN TALK ON THE KEY TRUTHS OF THE FAITH
Copyright © 1982 by The Zondervan Corporation
Grand Rapids, Michigan

Basic Training was originally published as *The Symbol,*
copyright © 1973 by The Presbyterian and Reformed Publishing Company. Copyright was transferred in 1981 to The
Zondervan Corporation. Revised 1982.

Library of Congress Cataloging in Publication Data

Sproul, R. C. (Robert Charles), 1939–
　　Basic training, plain talk on the key truths of the faith.

　　Rev. ed. of: The symbol. c1973.
　　Bibliography: p.
　　1. Theology, Doctrinal—Popular works. 2. Apostles'
Creed. I. Title.
BT77.S717　1982　　　238'.11　　　82-13564
ISBN 0-310-44921-9

The Scriptures used in this book are taken from the *New
American Standard Bible,* copyright © The Lockman Foundation, 1960, 1962, 1963, 1968, 1971, 1972. Used by permission.

Printed in the United States of America

　　83　84　85　86　87　88 — 10　9　8　7　6　5　4　3　2

TO VESTA

To the Romans, a pagan goddess;

to me, a godly wife.

Contents

The Apostles' Creed

I believe in God the Father Almighty, Maker of
    heaven and earth.
    And in Jesus Christ, His only Son, our Lord;
Who was conceived by the Holy Ghost, born of the
    virgin Mary;
    Suffered under Pontius Pilate; was crucified,
    dead, and buried; He descended into hell;
The third day He arose again from the dead;
    He ascended into heaven, and sitteth at the
    right hand of God the Father Almighty;
From whence He shall come to judge the quick and
    the dead.
    I believe in the Holy Ghost;
The Holy Catholic Church; the communion of
    saints;
    The forgiveness of sins;
The resurrection of the body;
    And the life everlasting. Amen.

Preface

This book was conceived as a response to the urgings of former college students of mine who indicated a desire for a basic treatment of the major tenets of classical Christianity. As a result, I have endeavored to set forth a contemporary exposition of the articles of the Apostles' Creed. This book is directed to a reading public of college students and intellectually-oriented laymen. Consequently, I have sought to adopt a semi-popular literary style, avoiding academic technicalia[1] as much as possible. I have sought in many cases to deal with highly complex theological matters in a manner that will simplify them for the reader.

The beginning student of theology must be cautioned against viewing this book as anything more than an introduction to theological questions. In seeking to simplify, I run the risk of distortion. Hopefully, that distortion is kept at a minimal level. I have sought to limit notations to those required by direct quotations and to note suggested volumes of further inquiry.

Many friends and colaborers have been helpful to me in the preparation of this volume. I am particularly indebted to Dr. Phillip Edgcumbe Hughes, and to Dr. John Gerstner for the suggestions and criticisms they have made of the manuscript. I am also grateful to Edna Gerstner (Mrs. John Gerstner) and Miss Nano Chalfant for rendering criticisms from the laymen's point of view. Special thanks go to Lucille Chevalier and Annette Rathbun for typing the manuscript.

---

[1]*Semper ubi, sub ubi.*

I Believe

When a person embraces the Christian faith and can say with assurance, "I believe . . . ," that person is embarking on a spiritual pilgrimage. The trip is one of adventure and excitement. It is also one that is fraught with many pitfalls, a journey full of surprises. At times the surprises that rear up and confront the Christian will startle or discourage him. The believer soon discovers that not everyone around him shares his excitement or his conviction. He finds that he is living in a world that is characterized largely by unbelief. His faith will be tested. It will face the fire of the crucible of life in a secular world. What is real of that faith will stand, but the dross will be burned away.

These are difficult times for the believer. The days in which we live are days characterized by skepticism, and rebuke is cast at those who walk by faith. It may be said that the days of sentimental faith are over. There is much preoccupation in our generation with the tragic and a mood of hopelessness is all too characteristic. There is a foreboding atmosphere that hovers over our culture—an atmosphere that looks to the future not with breathless anticipation and enthusiasm but rather with a sense of helplessness. To some the condition of the world is enough to call forth a renewed effort at faith. People do not want to abandon hope. The gates to our culture are similar to the gates of Dante's *Hell* and the pilgrim is discouraged because of the banner that stands over the future, "Abandon hope all ye who enter here."

The benevolent tranquility symbolized by the Eisenhower image that characterized the 50s crumbled beneath the upheaval and revolutions of the 60s. The 70s were a time of more disintegration of classical values and ideals and the decade of the 80s had an ominous beginning with the Soviet invasion of Afghanistan, the hostage crisis in Iran, and the bleak prospects of the future that hovered over the American economy so that the believer of the present is one whose faith must be based on reality. The faith must have a content.

In this hour of nonfaith for much of our culture, to say we believe with conviction seems to many to involve us in a fanciful flight into a make-believe world where stark reality is somehow softened by faith. Therefore the believer daily faces the questions of the skeptics and cynics. Is faith merely a leap into the absurd, a flight from reality, an exercise in outmoded religion? Is faith merely a bromide for the sick or a crutch for the weak? The question that many ask is whether religious faith is merely an escape route from reality. But the Christian confession, "I believe," has little to do with narcotics or fanciful imagination. The Christian is not interested in the absurd or the occult. Biblical Christianity knows nothing of "blind faith." Blindness, in biblical categories, is the mark of the unbelieving mind, not of the believer. There is a clear contrast between the confession of faith of a Christian and that of a "tiny Alice who closes her eyes and holds her breath, hoping to wish her desires into fulfillment." Faith for the Christian is not merely a projection of desires nor the creative power of the imagination. Rather, faith in the New Testament sense begins as a response; a response to a divine summons and activity.

Frequently we hear an appeal for Christians to live

by a simple faith. What do we mean when we speak of a simple faith? For faith to be simple it must be readily understood, clearly communicable, and sharply focused on its object. In that sense faith should be simple. However, it is easy to confuse a simple faith that is characterized by a childlike trust in the fidelity of God Himself, and a simplistic faith that under analysis yields only superstition. When we look to the Bible we see that faith, though simple, is at the same time complex. It is like a radiating diamond, simple in its refulgent splendor and beauty, but complex with its many particular facets. When the New Testament speaks of faith it speaks of something that has many dimensions to it. There is an intellectual dimension of faith, there is a sense in which faith touches heavily the human will, and there is an element of faith that is intimately bound up with our human emotions.

Faith and the Mind

History has produced many advocates of the idea that faith is basically something that is nonrational, something that has to do only with the heart and not at all with the mind. Tertullian early propounded the idea that to believe something because it is absurd is a noble thing to do. Now it is true that a certain amount of courage is required to believe what we think is absurd. But we wonder what the relationship is between discretion and valor in such a scheme. Tertullian is not too far removed from many contemporary thinkers who call us to a kind of blind faith in the midst of meaninglessness. This may be courageous but it is this kind of "faith" that is far removed from the New Testament concept.

The New Testament does not call us to crucify our intellect. There is no appeal to arbitrary decisions or choices. A call to faith in the New Testament is not an invitation to embrace contradictions and irrationality. To be sure the believer is often faced with mystery, with unknown dimensions that stretch far beyond the reach of his mind. But he is called to trust in that which is revealed and has been made known by the Scriptures. Crucifixion is always necessary in the Christian life, but it is our pride and our selfish will that must be crucified, not the mind. The New Testament does not elevate irrationality and incoherency as religious values. Incoherency is never the mark of God. The Holy Spirit is not confused. The hope that bears the Christian along in the midst of crisis is not borne merely of irrational determination that comes from clenched fists and gritted teeth whereby we determine to persevere in spite of the hopelessness of our life. Rather, the Christian takes his point of departure from the words of Jesus, "Be of good cheer, I have overcome the world" (John 16:33). Here Jesus does not call His people to an unreasonable act of courage or an irrational basis for hope. He gives a reason for His optimism; namely that He has overcome the world. If indeed Christ has overcome the world and He invites us to participate in that victory it would be irrational not to be of good cheer.

Thus faith is reasonable. That is not to say that faith is to be confused with rationalism, which gives a too one-sided emphasis on the mind's ability to understand all reality unaided. Nor is faith so one-sided that it obscures noncognitive elements of it. But truth is always involved with the mind. Truth may be truth without ever touching my mind or my understanding, but if it is ever to touch my life at some point I must have understanding.

Much has been said about faith being a verb rather than a noun, that is, modern forms of activism seek to place more emphasis on the doing of faith rather than on the thinking about faith. This emphasis on the vital application of faith to real human situations is a necessary one, but it is also a very dangerous one as it could lead us into a false dichotomy.

In biblical terms there is an escapable relationship

between my act of believing and the content of what it is I believe. Faith does not exist, indeed it cannot exist, in a vacuum. There is always a connection between myself as a believer and the content that is the object of my faith. The Apostles' Creed begins with the statement "I believe." However, it is important to note it does not end with that statement. As soon as the believer says he believes he goes on to say what it is that he believes. Thus the New Testament does not call us to faith in general but to faith in particular, namely to faith in a person and in the work of Jesus Christ.

At the time of the Reformation the question of the nature of faith was a burning issue that accompanied the larger theological debate of justification by faith alone. If justification is by faith alone then it is vitally important for the Christian to understand what faith really is and what kind of faith it is that brings him into a state of justification. The Christian leaders of that era were careful to define various aspects of faith that together make up that whole which is necessary for salvation. It was popular in the sixteenth century to isolate three vital aspects of saving faith as including (1) content, (2) intellectual assent, (3) personal trust. The first, intellectual content, has to do with the information communicated by the Bible and by the preaching of the early church to what it is we are called to believe. Here the information or the content includes the idea that God exists, that He has entered the world by incarnation in the person of Christ and that in Christ, the God-man, our redemption is secured through His work of death, resurrection, and ascension. For me to believe in Jesus I must first have some understanding of who He is and what He is all about. Therefore faith includes this content or the message of the New Testament. Now it is perfectly possible for someone to hear the message, have a clear understanding of it, and not agree that the message is in fact true. To be aware of the content and to disclaim its truth is to be in a state of unbelief. But to be a believer one must first be aware of this content. The second step that the Reformers indicated is also vital. A person must not only be aware of the content of faith to be a believer but must also give mental assent to the truth of this content. Thus, to be a Christian, I must not only know that Jesus died on the cross, but I must believe in fact it is true that He died as an atonement act. Here my mind must regard as true the content of the faith if I am to be truly a believer.

But what if I have all the content straight and clearly understand in my mind and am willing to acknowledge that all of this is indeed true. Does that in and of itself give me saving faith? Certainly not according to the Bible. The Bible acknowledges that it is possible for a person to have a perfect grasp of theology and even to be persuaded of the truth of that theology and still be barred from the kingdom. It is interesting to note that the first beings to recognize the true identity of Jesus were not the faithful Jews who surrounded Him as disciples, but were the demons who perceived the reality of the incarnate son of God, penetrating His cloak and disguise of the incarnate One and recognizing instantly that He was the son of the most high God. At this level we see that it is possible for the devils to know the truth of God and still hate what it is that that truth represents. The apostle James labors this point in his discussion concerning the difference between dead faith and vital faith. He writes:

> You believe that God is one. You do well; the demons also believe, and shudder. But are you willing to recognize, you foolish fellow, that faith without works is useless? (James 2:19–20)

Here sarcasm virtually drips from the apostle's pen. James clearly indicates that faith involves far more than mental assent. To give the assent of one's intellect to the things of God may elevate a person from the status of rank pagan to the status of the demon, but it does not bring that person into the kingdom of God. Satan assents to the facts, but he does not possess faith in the saving sense of the word. Therefore a person may have the mental dimension of faith and still be outside a living and loving relationship with God; that is possible only through faith. Thus the New Testament teaches that faith does have a mental dimension that is indispensable to the fullness of faith, but that as a singular dimension it cannot stand alone or be a substitute for the fullness of the total reality of faith.

Faith as a Disposition of the Heart

Although faith has to have a content if it is to be meaningful and if it involves the mind in a serious way, there nevertheless remains a vital personal aspect that is not exhausted by the above. This personal aspect may be described as the disposition or inclination of the heart toward Christ. Broadly stated this may simply be called love. Love, however, is so broad in its scope and contains so many mixed nuances that we need to sharpen our understanding of it in terms of our attitude toward God.

The Old Testament psalmist distinguished between the godly and ungodly person precisely in terms of the focus of one's delight. It is the godly person who delights in the things of God. His heart is inclined toward God. He embraces with joy the sovereignty of God. The ungodly person, by contrast, is described in terms of personal estrangement and hostility. His heart remains removed or at a distance from God. Alluding to the Old Testament, Jesus used the phrase, "This people honors Me with their lips, but their heart is far away from Me" (Matt. 15:8). People of faith set their hearts toward God; they pursue, they seek, they press into the kingdom. Those without true faith remain indifferent, aloof, or hostile toward God. This negative posture of disinclination may not be equated simply

17

with a lack of mental aspect and deals with the attitude of the heart. Therefore faith involves more than being persuaded of truth. It involves *loving the truth.* It means more than assenting to Christ; it means delighting in Him. Faith—true faith—loves the exaltation of Christ.

Faith and Superstition

Many well-meaning persons in our day have in their excitement about the discovery of Christian faith confused biblical faith with certain elements of superstition. Countless new Christians have gone through severe crises of faith when they discovered that some of the promises made to them by well-meaning evangelists did not conform to the reality of life. Speaking from a perspective of enthusiasm some preachers have maintained, "Come to Jesus and all your problems will be over." A troubled person hears such a message and responds to that preaching, expecting upon conversion to live a life without problems. Such scenes, which are repeated every day in the Christian world, are an occasion for much grief and bitter disappointment. There is a certain sense in which life does not become truly complicated until we embark on the pilgrimage of faith with Christ. Suddenly as a new Christian we discover that the game is being played for keeps. Suddenly ethical issues that before left the seared conscience untouched now play heavily on a newly sensitized conscience. Promises that preachers make that "Christians will never be sick" or "Christians will never suffer" or "Christians will always prosper" are shattered when people discover that in spite of their faith they must go through the valley of the shadow of death. They must experience the full reality of tragic disease and even loss of personal prosperity on certain occasions. If we think that God has promised us a life of prosperity free from sickness and free from tragedy and then encounter one of those problems, we are inclined

18

to have a crisis of faith by being confused as to why God has abandoned us. A biblically informed faith, however, overcomes such superstition as we understand that on page after page of the Bible Christians are told that in this world we must suffer many things, that we must know tribulation, that there will be times when we must participate in the humiliation of Christ Himself. Christ never promises freedom from death and pain in this world, but He does promise us His presence in the midst of these difficulties. It is superstition that robs faith of its muscle. Superstition sugarcoats the call to suffering that is a part of the gospel of Christ. It is superstition that cheapens the cost of discipleship and woos and entices the Christian with phony promises of superficial grace. True faith is a faith that calls for discipline, for courage, for endurance, for growth, in order that we may face with triumph the difficulties that surround us in the pilgrimage of life.

Faith and Works

The Epistle of James differentiates between vital faith and dead faith. This difference is really between true faith and false faith. The dead faith or false faith is in fact no faith at all. True faith manifests itself always in terms of works. It is works that is the test that divides real faith from a mere profession of faith. It is works that proves to us to be the test of obedience. Abraham's response to God's command to sacrifice his beloved son Isaac is cited by James as a model for true faith. Abraham here is vindicated as a man of true faith when he manifests and shows his faith by his actions. This does not mean that good works, objectively considered, necessarily indicate the presence of faith, but it means that where true faith is present, good works will inevitably follow. Obedience is the fruit of faith. Without obedience faith is shown to be false. Jesus stated it like this, "If you love me, keep my commandments."

19

Faith then has to do with fidelity. That is, we are called not only to be believing but also faithful to God. Being translated, that simply means that our lives are to be characterized by commandment keeping. To be sure our justification occurs when we are linked to Christ by faith. Our justification is not caused by good works, but it is important for us to remember that justification marks the beginning of the Christian life, not the end of it. The faith that justifies is a kind of faith that inevitably results in holy living. When true faith is present a new desire is quickened in the heart of people for obedience. This obedience does not occur overnight, but through a long process of maturing we begin more and more to conform to the will of Christ.

The life of Jesus is the New Testament model for faith. Where the saints of the Old Testament are often recalled as examples of faithful men such as Abraham, Elijah, etc., these heroes are all dwarfed by the comparative standard found in Jesus Himself. In Him, fidelity to the father is an all-consuming passion whereby Jesus regarded the doing of the Father's will His "meat and drink."

Faith involves living. It is more than professing and more than understanding theology. In the final analysis it involves commitment to the will of God. Faith has a content that fills the mind and grasps the heart to the end that a changed life is apparent. The end of faith is fidelity to Jesus Christ.

Faith and Confession of Faith

Through creedal statements and confessional formulas the church has sought to articulate the content of her faith in every age. Debates and even wars have been waged over controversies surrounding such creeds. In many cases, yesterday's creed has become today's museum piece. Confessions have come and gone and have been more or less relevant to their own subsequent generations, but there is no creedal statement that has endured so many centuries and so many battles as the Apostles' Creed. The enduring capacity of this creed is surely tied to its simplicity, its succinctness, and its clear focus on the most central affirmations of Christianity. The following chapters are intended to be a contemporary explanation of the Apostles' Creed; that is, the primary concern is not simply to give a historical exposition of each point of the creed but rather to deal with its basic tenets in light of the modern issues that surround it. If the church is to be the church she must always be a confessing body. The content of her faith remains a crucial matter, because as Christians we believe.

Chapter 2

In God

Not too long ago, a Christian businessman asked me the following question: "What do you think is the most important question that the modern secular person needs to have answered?" I replied to the query, "That's easy. The most important thing for modern secular people to understand is *who* God is." Note it's not so much the issue *that* God is, that is at stake, but it is God's identity, His nature, His personality that is most severely obscured in our day. The gentleman then went on to ask me a second question, "Well, what do you think is the most important question that Christians need to have answered for them in the twentieth century?" I replied, "That's easy, too. What Christians need to know is who God is; His personality, His identity, His nature." The man was puzzled by my response saying, "Isn't it clear that before a person can even be a Christian he must have some idea of who God is?" Of course, the man's observation was true. No one can come to Christ without having some knowledge of who God is, but the depth of our knowledge, the aspect of our knowledge that seems to be so lacking in our day, is in fact a deeper knowledge of God the Father. Volumes and volumes have been written on the person and work of Christ. A number of books have been written in the last two decades on the person and work of God the Holy Spirit. Surely it is vital for the Christian to understand Jesus and the Holy Spirit but both Jesus and the Holy Spirit are sent from the Father and are very much concerned about revealing to us the nature of the Father. And yet their work, their priority of showing us the Father, has often not been the priority of the church.

Recently I was pained to hear a woman say to me that when she goes to church her deepest desire is to be brought into the presence of God—to have her vision of God extended that she might worship Him more fervently. But she went on to say that it seems more and more that as she goes to church the nature of God is being hidden from her. God becomes obscured rather than revealed. She said, "Sometimes I wonder if the preachers do that on purpose so as not to confront us with some of the frightening or demanding aspects of the nature of God." The woman was heartbroken because she had a passionate desire to know God as He is, and Christians must know who God is if they are to grow in their worship and obedience.

One of the most critical controversies of our day has been the debate over the so-called "God-talk question." The issue has been raised, "Can we speak meaningfully about God at all?" Does the word God refer to something real that exists apart from man or does the word "God" simply refer to some inner aspect of man himself? Were the philosophers of the nineteenth century correct when they said that theology is really nothing more than warmed over anthropology and the idea of God is nothing more than a conglomerate of human attributes extended to the nth degree and really a vision of some kind of superman? What is God really like? Is He personal or only an impersonal higher force or vague ultimate reality?

God and Ice-Cream Cones

To sharpen our understanding of the God-talk problem, perhaps it would be helpful to illustrate it by a simple experiment.

I have used the following experiment on people of all age groups and theological sophistication; from seventh-grade communicant classes to seminary seniors, and, surprisingly, the results have varied little. I have asked the students to close their eyes and think in concrete images about their favorite ice-cream cone. After they contemplate for awhile, I then ask what flavor of cone they are visualizing. The answers vary from person to person, from pistachio nut to raspberry ripple. A summary of the flavors mentioned usually resembles the list posted over the counter in a Howard Johnson's restaurant. The conclusion we reach is that contemplating ice-cream cones in concrete terms is not really difficult.

However, the situation becomes complicated when we move from the realm of ice cream to the realm of theology. I ask the students to repeat the experiment, but this time to think concretely, not of ice-cream cones, but of God. The further stipulation is that they visualize not God the Son, nor God the Holy Spirit, but specifically God the Father. Inevitably, there are those who cannot move from abstract thinking to concrete thinking and who respond by saying that they visualize "love." Of course, "love" is as abstract as "God" and gives us very little insight concretely into what or who God is. What these people are saying is that the word "God" evokes similar feeling or association as the word "love." This association is helpful to our understanding of our personal relationship to God, but adds little to concrete imagination. Most people, however, are able to conjure up a mental image in association with the word "God." It is at this point that there is little difference between the imagination of the child and the scholar. Some of the images expressed include the following: an old man with a beard sitting on a white throne; a gray cloud of smoke; a red button on a massive instrument panel; a member of the person's family; Michelangelo's painting of Creation on the ceiling of the Sistine

Chapel; a volcanic eruption; a nuclear explosion; lightning flashing across an ominous black sky; a brilliant white light; a giant brain; an old man with tears in his eyes. The catalog could continue. However, these are enough to demonstrate that people have widely varied mental images of God.

After this experiment is done in a group, I ask the question, "How many of you think that God *is* a cloud of smoke, a volcanic eruption, a giant brain, etc.?" In every situation where I have asked the question, the response has been unanimous. No one thought that God could be absolutely identified with any one or all of the descriptions. Yet the people felt that the images mentioned were not nonsensical, but communicated effectively (though not totally) something meaningful about God. For these people the term "God" was hazy and ambiguous, yet not empty of meaning.

If we analyze the catalog of images mentioned above, we can find some very important basic similarities. All are descriptions of God in human terms, by forms common to our existence as people. What happens is that God is thought of *analogically.* The people found some kind of analogy between God and white light, red buttons, etc., yet realized that God could not be tied to the analogy. Another interesting observation may be seen in the fact that many of the images mentioned were similar to biblical images of God.

Analogical Speaking of God

Thomas Aquinas differentiated between three types of descriptive uses of language. The first type is the univocal use of language. This is the use of a descriptive term where the term is applied to two different things and means basically the same thing. For example, the word "bald" when applied to men and to eagles means substantially the same thing. The phrase, "the man is bald," means virtually the same thing as the phrase, "the eagle is bald." That is, the term "bald" in both cases means the absence of hair on the head. (The question of whether the eagle is *really* bald is irrelevant to the discussion of the *use* of the term "bald" as it is commonly done with reference to eagles.) Thus, univocal language is language used to describe two different levels of being where the meaning of the term does not change in proportion to the difference of the beings described.

The equivocal use of language is that use where the meaning of a term changes radically when applied to two different orders of reality. (Equivocation is a common cause of logical fallacies.) For example, suppose a college student attended a dramatic reading program, and, upon his return to his dormitory, he told his roommate it was a "bald" narrative. What would he mean? Would he mean that the narrative didn't have hair on its head? Obviously not, as a narrative has neither head nor hair (some contemporary plays notwithstanding). Does this mean, then, that the term "bald" when applied to a narrative is utterly meaningless? No. In the equivocal use of the term "bald" in this case, there remains a point of contact with physical baldness, as remote as that contact may be. What the student was saying was that something was *lacking* in the narrative. Probably it was very dull and unexciting, and, as a bald man lacks hair, so the narrative lacked dynamic punch and was "bald." Hence, equivocal language is that language where the meaning of the term changes radically when applied to two different realms.

Aquinas maintained that when we speak of God we use neither univocal nor equivocal language. To think that our theological vocabulary is univocal is to fail to understand the qualitative difference between the creature and Creator. It fails to take seriously the transcendent otherness of God. His ways are not our ways. We can never identify God in a univocal sense with anything created. We must respect what the theologians call the *Deus Absconditus* (the hidden aspect of God).

To speak univocally of God is to reduce theology to anthropology and to fall under the devastating critique of Feuerbach. At the same time, our knowledge of God is not so destitute that we can only speak of Him equivocally. Where univocal thinking fails to do justice to the hidden aspect of God, equivocal thinking fails to do justice to the *Deus Revelatus* (the revealed aspect of God). Univocal language assumes too much similarity between God and man; equivocal language assumes too little.

For Aquinas, the most meaningful method of God-talk is the analogical. Analogical language involves the use of terms whose meanings change proportionately to the difference of the beings described. An example may be seen in the common use of the word "good." We speak of a good man and a good dog. A good dog is one that is probably obedient to his master, does not bite people, is housebroken, etc. When we call a man good, we mean considerably more than that he is housebroken and that he does not go around biting people, etc. Obviously, "good" does not mean the same thing when applied to men as it does when applied to dogs. Yet the meaning is not so far removed as to be called equivocal. The term "good" when applied to dogs and men has a greater point of contact than the term "bald" has when applied to men and narratives. Analogical language is more meaningful than equivocal, though less meaningful than univocal. It is the analogical method that must be used in God-talk. Analogical language protects the borders of the *Deus Absconditus* and the *Deus Revelatus*. It assumes neither too much, nor too little. It does not provide a total and exhaustive comprehension of God, neither does it leave us in hopeless ignorance. Aquinas' most emphatic point is that analogical language provides us with an adequate and meaningful method of God-talk, though not a total and exhaustive method. The ground basis for such analogical talk is creation and history.

The Way of Negation

Because of the problem of our inability to describe God univocally, some have argued that we cannot say anything positive about God. All we can say about God is what He is not. The classic proponent of such a negative view was the neo-Platonist philosopher, Plotinus. For Plotinus, God, or "The One," is totally unknowable except by mystical experience that gives no rationally communicable content:

> He that would speak exactly must not name it by this name or by that; we can but circle, as it were, about its circumference seeking to interpret in speech our experience of it, now shooting near the mark, and again disappointed of our aim by reason of the antinomies we find in it.[1]

It was the incomprehensibility of God that occupied much of Melville's reflection in *Moby Dick*. Here the whale in its awesome "whiteness" manifested the ambiguity of God. Ishmael wondered:

> Is it that by its indefiniteness it shadows forth the heartless voids and immensities of the universe, and thus stabs us from behind with the thought of annihilation, when beholding the white depths of the milky way? Or is it, that as in essence whiteness is not so much a color as the visible absence of color, and at the same time the concrete of all colors; is it for these reasons that there is such a dumb blankness, full of meaning, in which a wide landscape of snows—a colorless, all-color of atheism from which we shrink? . . . Pondering all this, the palsied universe lies before us a leper; and like willful travelers in Lapland, who refuse to wear colored and coloring glasses upon their eyes, so the wretched infidel gazes himself blind at the monumental white shroud that wraps all the prospect around him. And of all these things the Albino

---

[1]Enneads, VI, ix, 3, 4.

whale was the symbol. Wonder ye then at the fiery hunt?[2]

The value of the way of negation is in that it serves to protect us from assuming our knowledge of God is greater than it is. It reminds us of the *Deus Absconditus* (the hidden, unrevealed aspect of God). It prohibits us from giving univocal import to analogical descriptions. It emphasizes that "His ways are not our ways, and his ways are past finding out." With David we cry, "Such knowledge is too wonderful for us. . . . It is too high—I cannot attain to it" (Ps. 139:6).

The Way of Affirmation

As valuable as the way of negation may be in serving as a necessary balance, it is not the only or primary way of the Christian. The believer is not left in a dismal abyss of incomprehensibility. Our God has not left us in darkness. There is no place in the Christian church for a monument TO AN UNKNOWN GOD. To reduce Christianity to total negation is to side with the fool. Luther stated with boldness:

> To take no pleasure in assertions is not the mark of a Christian heart; indeed, one must delight in assertions to be a Christian at all. . . . Away, now, with Sceptics and Academics from the company of us Christians; let us have men who will assert, men twice as inflexible as very Stoics! Nothing is more familiar or characteristic among Christians than assertion. Take away assertions, and you take away Christianity. . . . The Holy Spirit is no Sceptic, and the things He has written in our hearts are not doubts or opinions, but assertions—surer and more certain than sense and life itself.[3]

---

[2]Herman Melville, *Moby Dick*, ed. Alfred Kazin (Cambridge: Mass.: Riverside Press, 1956) p. 161.

[3]Martin Luther, *The Bondage of the Will* (Westwood, N.J.: Revell, 1957), pp. 69–70.

To deny what we do know on the basis of what we do not know is not only bad theology, but also bad science. A one-sided emphasis of the *Deus Absconditus* fails to do justice to the *Deus Revelatus* (that aspect of God which is revealed). So the church has proclaimed and confessed that knowledge of God is not only possible, but God can be adequately known and communicated.

Naming God

One of the most significant ways of speaking about God is by means of His name. The third commandment of the Decalogue prohibits the desecration of the name of God. The first petition of the Lord's Prayer is that the name of God be *hallowed.* There is a unique and inseparable connection between God and His name. To use the name of God flippantly or as a curse word is to manifest a gross disrespect for God Himself. The Jews' reticence to utter the ineffable name did not arise out of a superstitious view that projected magical power to a name, but rather from a holy respect for the God of the name. God's name is holy because He is holy.

The close relationship between person and name that is found throughout the Bible is not entirely foreign to us. This can be illustrated by an episode that took place in a college classroom. A young co-ed entered the class one morning in an obvious state of delight and enthusiasm. A diamond ring on her left hand and the dreamy gaze she directed to the young man seated beside her made the reason for her delight abundantly obvious. I put her on the spot by asking, "Mary, did you just get engaged?" When she answered in the affirmative, I said to her, "Would you mind if I inferred from the fact that you are engaged to John that you are also in love with John?" She allowed the inference! I then proceeded to ask Mary if she would be willing to tell the class precisely why she was in love with John. She responded enthusiastically that it was because he was so handsome. At this, I pointed to Bill, who recently had been elected escort to the campus queen, and asked Mary if she also thought Bill was handsome. When she replied positively, I pointed out that perhaps there was something else about John that made her prefer him to Bill. She was quick to add that John was athletic. During this, Bill sat in the back of the room wearing a varsity sweater adorned with letters in three major sports. When I called Mary's attention to that, she hastily added that John was intelligent. Bill began to grin as he knew I would quickly mention his being president of the academic honor society. By this time, Mary was beginning to manifest frustration, and, as the interrogation proceeded, she singled out John's propensity for courtesy as a factor that moved her to love. I asked Mary, "Are you suggesting that Bill is rude?" By this time the class was hysterical and thoroughly enjoying Mary's rising crescendo of frustration. (I would not recommend duplicating this experiment unless you find a "Mary" who is an exceedingly good sport!) To spare Mary any further discomfort, I asked her to bring the issue to a close by naming precisely and definitively what quality most attracted her to John. She said, "I love him because he's. . . , because he's. . . because, ah. . . because he's John!" Instantly, the class became sober as they realized what had happened. When Mary failed to capture the uniqueness of John by listing his attributes, she resorted ultimately to his name. For the name "John" meant to Mary, not merely a cipher on a birth certificate, but a symbol of all that he was and the whole history of their relationship.

The Christian faith does not involve belief in God-in-general. The Christian is not a theist, but a Yahwist. That is, our hope rests not in a "supreme being," but in the God and Father of our Lord Jesus Christ. He is not known to us via abstract speculation, but is revealed to us in concrete acts of history. The one who revealed Himself to Moses gave "I AM THAT I AM" as a name, not a definition. Emil Brunner points out:

> But the Name of God is only a "proper Name" be-
> cause it does not stand alongside of a general con-
> ception, of an appellation. The plural "gods" is an
> insult to God; it belongs to the Nature of God that
> there should be "none other beside Him!"[4]

Thus, the God of Scripture is, "The God who. . . ."
He is called the God of Abraham, Isaac, and Jacob; the
One who did this or did that. He reveals Himself
through His divine activity in the history of His people.
The history of God's self-revelation, however, is not
confined to redemptive history, but has its roots in
creation. Quite apart from the special revelation of Israel's history, God manifests Himself in and through
His creation. The psalmist says, "The heavens are telling of the glory of God; and their expanse is declaring
the work of His hands" (Ps. 19:1). Paul maintained,
"For since the creation of the world His invisible attributes, namely, His eternal power and divine nature,
have been clearly seen" (Rom. 1:20).

Thus, God is known generally in creation and
specifically in the events of redemptive history. God is
not known, however, simply in the naked events of this
history. He does not just work and leave it up to our
speculation to discover who is working and what is
being said in the event. God not only acts, but He
speaks through the mouths of His prophets and apostles. The Scriptures are therefore the normative source
of special revelation because they provide not only a
record of God's acts, but also an inspired interpretation
of those acts. It is because of this quality of Scripture
that Jesus called the prophets and the apostles the
foundation of the church. Any attempt to isolate the
biblical record of events from the biblical interpretation
of the events must lead to despair. To make such a
separation is to leave us with naked events that take on

---

[4]Emil Brunner, *The Christian Doctrine of God,* Dogmatics: I
(Philadelphia: Westminster Press, 1950), p. 123.

the character of a chameleon, changing its color with every fantasy of the interpreter.

The zenith of God's self-revelation is found in the person and work of Christ, the "Logos," who is also called the one who "is the radiance of His glory and the exact representation of His nature, and upholds all things by the word of His power" (Heb. 1:3). God's supreme revelation of Himself is the Incarnation, the Word becoming flesh and speaking to us at our level of understanding. It was Philip who said to Jesus, "Lord, show us the Father, and it is enough for us." If ever the reader of the text can detect a note of impatience or frustration in the words of Jesus, it must be in His reply to Philip's request. "Have I been so long with you, and yet you have not come to know me, Philip? He who has seen Me has seen the Father; how do you say, 'Show us the Father'?" (John 14:8-10). The staggering statement, "He who has seen Me has seen the Father," forms the ground basis for all Christian talk about God. It is the Incarnation that drives the Christian from the way of negation to a glorious way of affirmation.

Concrete and Abstract Language

Many attempts have been made in history to sharpen and refine our language of God in order to transcend the barrier posed in the tension between the *Deus Absconditus* and the *Deus Revelatus*. Philosophical terminology has been helpful to the scholar but often has led to the confusion of univocal and analogical language. By abstract language we have often thought we have penetrated the very essence of God. Some have even attempted to seek a "God beyond God" to escape the dilemma. Unfortunately, there is no God beyond God and to attempt to transcend the analogical limits of human speech requires first that we transcend our own humanity. All of our language is anthropomorphic because we are all *anthropoi!* All human talk of God must be rejected if we attach univocal weight to it. But

33

it is not necessary to speak univocally to speak meaningfully.

Helmut Gollwitzer has properly stated that particular and concrete ways of speaking have the preference over general and abstract ones; and personal ways of speaking have the preference over impersonal, neuter ones.[5] To speak with concrete and simple images has the advantage of making it obvious that our images are not to be taken univocally. When God asks Moses, "Is the LORD'S power limited?" (Num. 11:23), He is saying, in effect, "Moses, are you dealing with a divine cripple? Do I have a withered arm?" Here God speaks clearly and graphically of His overwhelming power. The concept of "arm of the Lord" is a frequent image in the Bible that communicates simply, but meaningfully.

When we are told of God, that ". . . the cattle on a thousand hills are His," we are clearly not being told that God is the "Great Rancher in the Sky" who occasionally has a shoot-out with Satan at the O. K. Corral. We are being told that God claims ownership over His creation and we are to bow to His authority. The simpler the image, the less likely the confusion.

We confess, "I believe in God. . . ." That confession is not an expression of creative imagination or projection, but is a response to the One who manifests Himself in creation, in history, in deed and in word, and supremely in Christ. Our talk of Him is legitimate because He has entered into the arena of human activity. We confess not only that there is a God, but that God can be known and our knowledge of Him can be meaningfully communicated.

Process Theology

Another trend in contemporary thought is process theology. Although such advocates of this position as

---

[5]Helmut Gollwitzer, *The Existence of God as Confessed by Faith* (Philadelphia: Westminster Press), p. 153.

Whitehead, Hartshorne, Robb, and Ogden differ on various intramural questions, they are agreed on a number of central points. They unanimously reject the God of classical Christianity. They believe that God is involved in a continual process of change. God is said to have two poles, potential and actual. The potential pole is infinite and the actual pole is finite. Thus God is potentially infinite but actually finite. The potential pole is beyond this world and the actual pole is in the physical world. As a soul is related to the body, so God is related to the world. The world is God's body. The world depends on God for direction and God depends on the world for growth in perfection. Human beings by their effort can contribute to God's growth in value and perfection. Because God is finite there is no guarantee that evil will ultimately be defeated. It will actually never be possible to overcome all evil.

Process theology is an intricate system involving much philosophical terminology and argumentation. It is in radical opposition to the biblical God. God is reduced to a director who participates in the world process rather than the sovereign Creator. God is seen as continually becoming more perfect rather than having all perfections. God is seen as being unable to conquer evil, rather than the One who will ultimately defeat all evil. The God of process theology is a long way from "God the Father Almighty" who has been worshiped throughout the ages.

Chapter 3

The Father Almighty

The fatherhood of God has been a source of much controversy in the history of the Christian church. In eighteenth-century America, Unitarianism emerged as a conscious alternative to classical Christianity. At the heart of the Unitarian creed was the idea of the universal fatherhood of God and brotherhood of man. The same universal sense of fatherhood was an integral part of the nineteenth-century liberal Christianity. The use of the science of comparative religion prompted numerous efforts to distill "essences" from various world religions. This was done mainly to seek a basic common denominator that could be found to unite (at least conceptually) the variant religions of the world. If it could be shown that God was the Father of all men, then it would follow that all men are brothers and none could claim exclusive knowledge or privilege from the Father.

The New Testament does recognize a broad sense in which God is the Father of all men, but this is only a secondary usage of the term "Father" and not the primary one. Paul, at Mars Hill, alludes to the universal fatherhood of God when he says:

> And He made from one, every nation of mankind to live on all the face of the earth, having determined their appointed times, and the boundaries of their habitation, that they should seek God, if perhaps

they might grope for Him and find Him, though He is not far from each one of us; for in Him we live and move and exist, as even some of your own poets have said, "For we also are His offspring" (Acts 17:26–28).

In this instance Paul acknowledges that all men are the "offspring" of God in the sense that we are all dependent on God for our origin and continuity of existence. As Creator, God is the ultimate progenitor. Also, God gives His common grace liberally to all men. His rain falls on the just as well as on the unjust. However, in biblical categories, to call on God as Father involves far more than acknowledging His powers of creation or His control of the universe. Primarily, it has reference to a unique personal filial relationship that is not assumed outside of a relationship with Christ. The question of sonship and fatherhood was a critical and stormy issue between Jesus and His contemporaries. To escape the indictment Jesus directed against their bondage to sin, the Jews first appealed to their relationship with Abraham. "Abraham is our father." But Jesus replied, "If you are Abraham's children, do the deeds of Abraham. But as it is, you are seeking to kill Me, a man who has told you the truth which I heard from God; this Abraham did not do." They said to Him, "We were not born of fornication; we have one Father, even God." Jesus said to them, "If God were your Father, you would love Me; for I proceeded forth and have come from God, for I have not even come on My own initiative, but He sent Me. Why do you not understand what I am saying? It is because you cannot hear My word. You are of your father the devil, and you want to do the desires of your father" (John 8:39–44).

Here Jesus clearly disputes any concept of a universal fatherhood of God. For Jesus, sonship is inseparably related to obedience. We are the children of those whom we love and serve. To honor the Father is to honor the Son. To claim God as Father and at the same time disavow the Son is to miss the point of the biblical view of fatherhood. Jesus said, "He who does not honor the Son does not honor the Father who sent Him" (John 5:23). That narrow exclusiveness was a scandal to the Jews and has been a scandal ever since. The Bible does not define sonship in biological terms. There is a clearly implied spiritual distinction between the "children of light" and the "children of darkness." We are not born the children of God. It was Israel's gravest error to assume an automatic filial relationship with God on the basis of biology. Sonship comes through faith, not genetics. "We were," says Paul, "by nature children of wrath" (Eph. 2:3).

Spiritual Sonship

Nicodemus was bewildered when Jesus confronted him with the statement, "Truly, truly I say unto you, unless one is born again, he cannot see the kingdom of God . . . unless one is born of water and the Spirit, he cannot enter into the kingdom of God. That which is born of the flesh is flesh; and that which is born of the Spirit is spirit . . ." (John 3:3–6). Here Jesus relates sonship to regeneration. Sonship is not automatic, but comes through the work of the Holy Spirit. "But as many as received Him, to them He gave the right to become children of God, even to those who believe in His name, who were born not of blood, nor of the will of the flesh, nor of the will of man, but of God" (John 1:12–13). In this statement, sonship is seen as being inseparably related to faith and is accomplished not by human effort, heredity, or achievement. It is by the power of the Spirit that we become the children of God.

Perhaps this is most clearly seen in Paul's teaching regarding sonship in Romans 8:

> For all who are being led by the Spirit of God, these are sons of God. For you have not received a spirit of slavery leading to fear again, but you have received a spirit of adoption as sons by which we cry out,

"Abba! Father!" The Spirit Himself bears witness with our spirit that we are children of God, and if children, heirs also, heirs of God and fellow-heirs with Christ, if indeed we suffer with Him in order that we may also be glorified with Him (vv. 14–17).

To be able to cry "Abba" is the unspeakable privilege of the sons of God. When Jesus instructs His disciples to address God in prayer as "Our Father," He is sharing a unique privilege with His friends. To confess God as Father is not an act of presumption if one is in Christ, but it is the supreme doxology. In the word "Father" is contained the history of His paternal love and care for us. When we call on God as Father, we are not only giving God praise and honor, but we are acknowledging His authority over us.

The Brotherhood of Adoption

The Christian faith manifests a powerful force of fellowship. This fellowship is rooted in a strange type of brotherhood. While the New Testament calls us to love all men and to see all men as neighbors, brotherhood is focused in a peculiar relationship to Christ.[1] Christ alone is the Son of God in the ultimate sense. He is the "only-begotten." But in Him we are adopted into the family of God. We are brothers then with all the adopted sons who are joined to Christ. The brotherhood may be divided theologically or methodologically, but if the same Spirit is shared by all, then brotherhood exists.

Almighty

God is known to the Israelites as the Almighty One. That He is not simply "mighty," but "all"-mighty distinguishes Him from the spurious deities of the pagans. His power extends over all creation. He is not a

---

[1]For a more technical discussion of the New Testament meaning of brotherhood, see von Soden's article on "Adelphos" in Kittel's *Theological Dictionary of the New Testament,* Vol. I (Grand Rapids: Eerdmans, 1964).

storm god, though the storm indeed gives evidence of His awesome power. He is not a fertility god, yet He is in control of the seasons and climactic changes. He is not a god of war like Mars, but no army can contain His might. He is *all*-mighty.

When God's attributes are catalogued, He is usually described as omni-this and omni-that, i.e., omniscient, omnipotent, etc. God's omnipotence has been the target of many budding theologians who love to stump their professors with the supposedly unanswerable question, "Can God build a rock so big that He is unable to move it?" The horns of the dilemma are clear. If we answer Yes to the question, we are affirming that there is something God cannot do, i.e., move the rock. If we answer No, we are still saying there is something God cannot do, namely, build such a rock. Thus, say the tyrotheologians, no matter how we answer the question, we are forced to deny the omnipotence of God. Of course, the error implicit in this judgment rests on the false assumption that "omnipotence" when applied to God means, univocally, that God can do anything or everything. The word itself literally means omni—all and potence—power, or ability. Here is a crystal-clear example of how abstract terminology may lead us into theological hot water. The word "omnipotence" was never intended to suggest that God could do everything. The Scriptures speak forthrightly about certain things God cannot do. We are told that He cannot lie and that He cannot die. God cannot be God and not be God at the same time. He, in other words, cannot act contrary to His nature. This limitation, however, is not a limitation imposed on God by His creation, but is an intrinsic internal limitation of His own being. When the word "omnipotence" is understood in its proper theological sense, the problem of the rock quickly vanishes.

Omnipotence simply means that God is in control of His creation and that He exercises dominion over it.

That is, omnipotence does not describe God's nature so much as His *relationship* to the created order. If it is so understood, then the answer to the "unanswerable" question is obvious. No! God could not build a rock so big that He could not move it. To say that He could build such a rock is to say that there could be a part of the creation that was beyond the scope of God's control. That would deny His omnipotence. To say that God cannot build such a rock is not to deny His omnipotence, but to affirm it!

One of the special names the Israelites used to call on God was closely connected to His almighty power. The name *El Shaddai,* dating from patriarchal times, came from the verb "to overpower," "to be violated," or "to destroy." Some scholars find its origin in the words "the thunderer" or "the One who is sufficient," but the most probable meaning is "the One who overpowers."[2] Its frequent use in the Book of Job gives credence to this view. Job is overwhelmed by the awesome power of God manifested in the lengthy interrogation recorded in chapters 38–42. The might of God is revealed against all who would seek to overthrow Him. The psalmist portrays a summit meeting of the world powers who enter into a conspiracy against God:

> Why are nations in an uproar, and the peoples devising a vain thing? The kings of the earth take their stand, and the rulers take counsel together, against the Lord and against His anointed: "Let us tear their fetters apart, and cast away their cords from us" (Ps. 2:1–3).

The response of God to the combined forces of man united against Him is laughter! "He who sits in the heavens laughs!" The total might of men mustered against God is like the "mouse that roared." The foolishness of men in their war with God is matched

---

[2]Geerhardus Vos, *Biblical Theology* (Grand Rapids: Eerdmans, 1951), p. 96.

only by their arrogance. Elsewhere the psalmist declares, "The nations made an uproar, the kingdoms tottered; He raised His voice, the earth melted . . ." (Ps. 46:6). Here, one word from the lips of God is enough to melt the earth! It brings to mind the image of a man who annihilates an ant by one slight press of the thumb.

The image of God's might was not a picture of divine tyranny to the Jew, nor was it an expression of arbitrary sovereignty. It was one of the strongest assertions of Israel's true consolation. The God of Israel is not impotent, but manifests Himself as the King of Glory:

> Lift up your heads, O gates! and be lifted up, O ancient doors, that the King of glory may come in! Who is the King of glory? The LORD strong and mighty, The LORD mighty in battle. . . . Who is this King of glory? The LORD of hosts, He is the King of glory! (Ps. 24:7–10).

Chapter 4

Maker of Heaven and Earth

The question of man's purpose and destiny is closely related to the question of his origin. To confess that God is Creator is to confess that man is not a cosmic accident, devoid of any ultimate worth.

Creation or Chaos?

The twentieth century has brought a crisis to our understanding of man and his destiny. It is a time of kaleidoscopic change which carries with it chaotic confusion. A mood of restlessness bordering on despair permeates much of our civilization. The naïve optimism of nineteenth-century humanism has given way to various kinds of skepticism. The rise of atheistic existentialism has cast a shadow on discussions of the meaning of human existence.

Martin Heidegger has been one of the most significant voices of contemporary philosophy. He sees man trapped in the chaos of time. Man is conscious of the passing of time, but he is threatened by the fact that he does not know from where he has come and where he is going. Man is trapped in a state of what Heidegger calls "throwness"; that is, he feels that he has been chaotically hurled or thrown into life with the only certainty before him his own death. This situation provokes a feeling of "angst" or anxiety in the person. How a man deals with this anxiety determines how "authentic" his existence will be. If the person succumbs to this kind of anxiety, he destroys his authentic existence. Authentic existence is achieved only by the courage to live in freedom in spite of the ominous future. Life is ultimately meaningless. The only meaning there is, is the meaning the existential hero creates for himself. In this view, it is the creative power of man, not God, that gives any hope to life.

Similar strains are found in Frederick Nietzsche, who gave an earlier formulation to nihilism. It was Nietzsche who declared that God is dead and what is left is the *nihil* (nothingness). There are no values or purpose save what we create for ourselves. The inauthentic man flees into the security of the group and finds his solace in the morality of the herd. He becomes a slave to the herd lest he is forced to face the threat of the *nihil*.

Existentialism has done much to focus our attention on the naked realities of chaos that confront us in the human predicament. They have made it impossible to sweep the threatening aspects of human existence under some neatly-woven metaphysical rug. They have screamed a loud No! to all contrived systems that fail to take the human tragedy seriously. However, they leave us with no answer to chaos except a blind leap of faith or courage that is equally chaotic. If there are no values, then existentialism cannot have value. Perhaps the most consistent answer to chaos in existential terms would be silence. But, of course, the existentialist feels no need to be consistent. For him to be consistent would be to deny his own view of the chaotic.

Other answers have been provided for modern man's understanding of his predicament. From the mechanistic determinists and hyperevolutionists, we get some answer to the origin of man and some clue to his destiny. In this view, man is the highest point on the evolutionary scale of life that emerged out of the primordial slime. Man, the grown-up germ, is the result of cosmic accidental forces whose destiny is still in the hands of indifferent, impersonal forces. This view gives more insight into the origin of human existence and does not leave us in total darkness as to the goal of human existence as existentialism does. However, it also leaves us with a philosophy of insignificance, in that man begins in the slime and is destined for organic disorganization or disintegration. E. J. Carnell put it this way: "Modern man appears to be but a grown-up germ, sitting on a gear of a vast cosmic machine which is someday destined to cease functioning because of lack of power."[1]

This mechanistic view of man has failed to give us any understanding of the meaning of life. All kinds of attempts have been made to develop a sense of ethics that would relate to man in this system. All have failed. Why should germs be moral? If I am a cosmic accident, why should I "give a damn" about you? You are insignificant and so am I. Why should we prefer life over death? What is so special about life? Why should man be valued over a stone? More devastating to man than a hostile universe, is an indifferent one. With this kind of world view present today, is it any wonder why we ask Alfie, "What's it all about?"

The biblical view of creation is not one that retreats from coming to grips with the threat of chaos. In the Old Testament, the forces of chaos are closely linked with the symbol of the sea in general and the primordial sea monster in particular. Israel often contrasted the threatening power of the sea with the life-giving solace of the river. The violent storms that came from the Mediterranean Sea and the attacks of the seafaring Philistines were a constant source of danger to the Jew. In marked contrast, the Jordan gave the parched land

---

[1]Edward J. Carnell, *An Introduction to Christian Apologetics* (Grand Rapids: Eerdmans, 1948).

its life. Here, the river is the victory of life over death, of peace over violence and chaos. This contrast may be seen in Psalm 46:

> God is our refuge and strength, a very present help in trouble. Therefore we will not fear, though the earth should change, and though the mountains slip into the heart of the sea; though its waters roar and foam, though the mountains quake at its swelling tide. There is a river whose streams make glad the city of God, the holy dwelling places of the Most High. God is in the midst of her, she will not be moved; God will help her when morning dawns (vv. 1–5).

In ancient religion there is a recurrent image of the sea monster as the image of primordial chaos. Only in the religion of Israel is there ultimate victory over the forces of chaos. The opening of Genesis reads:

> In the beginning God created the heavens and the earth. And the earth was formless and void, and darkness was over the surface of the deep; and the Spirit of God was moving over the surface of the waters. Then God said, "Let there be light"; and there was light. And God saw that the light was good; . . ." (1:1–4).

In this passage, attention must be given to the description of the earth as being formless and void, with darkness on the face of the deep. The Spirit moves over the waters. Perhaps this indicates nothing more than the state of the as yet unordered, unfinished creation; or, as some have suggested, we have here a highly symbolical account of God's triumph over the forces of chaos. In any case, the fact is clear that God's power extends over the void and is not left in a Mexican stand-off with the forces of chaos. God's Spirit moves—and in the creative act the power of God is manifested with the consequent benediction: it was good!

The Christian confesses a God who has power far

greater than the forms of chaos. The serpent seduces man, but he cannot destroy him. Christianity knows no eternal dualism, but confesses the God who keeps the chaotic forces under control. God asks Job, "Can you draw out Leviathan with a fishhook? . . ." (Job 41:1). Here, the powerlessness of Job is set in marked contrast with the power of God. God's power over evil is so great that He goes fishing for the primordial sea monster and catches him with a five-pound test line!

The goal of creation is not chaos, but order. The Spirit moves over the waters, and out of the abyss and the void comes order. Out of the darkness comes the piercing light. The creation account moves in a rising crescendo through one day and then another until a moving climax is reached on the sixth day. On this day the crowning act of God's creation is reached: God creates man. It is the sixth day that has grasped our attention. We seem to be preoccupied with this day as we see nothing beyond the level of man.

Humanism as a Penultimate Solution

Humanism is not a recent phenomenon in history. Various forms of humanism have appeared throughout recorded history. It was the ancient philosopher Protagoras who issued the motto *Homo Mensura*, i.e., "Man is the measure."

In Protagoras's thinking, man was the yardstick of all virtue and ideals. The goal of creation was seen in that which most exalts man. Concern for man is at the heart of all forms of humanism. Since Christianity is also deeply concerned about man, it is often difficult to distinguish between Christianity and humanism. Both seek the healing of estranged relationships, and both seek the honoring of the dignity of man. However, the basis for dignity is radically different in humanism and Christianity. The Christian sees the horizontal relation of man to man as being inseparably related to the vertical relationship of God and man. To deal with man merely at the human, horizontal level is to neglect the vital basis of that horizontal relationship. The murder of Abel by Cain followed the violation of God's command in the garden situation. The estrangement was first vertical before it manifested itself horizontally. In Jesus' summary of the law, He appealed first to the Great Commandment, "Thou shalt love the Lord thy God with all thy heart" . . . and then "thy neighbor as thyself." Humanism isolates the latter from the former and, thus, leaves us with a penultimate solution.

How does humanism establish the dignity of man? Without the creation motif, the humanist is left with an arbitrary and irrational basis for man's dignity. If the origin of man is purposeless, why should dignity be ascribed to man? Apart from sentimental reasons, what reasons may be given for the assumption that man has any more dignity than a stone? Since the advent of the Christian faith in history, humanism has constantly incorporated much of the Christian ethic and value system, but has ripped the heart out of its theological context which alone can give sense to the ethic. As a man, I resent someone making moral demands on me and telling me I "ought" to do this or that without giving a reason. Human dignity and value cannot rest as mere "givens" of human experience. To be sure, our experience screams to us that life is valuable and that man is a creature of the highest worth and dignity, but that scream becomes a clanging symbol if, in fact, man is a germ with no destiny but death.

Sabbath Holiness as Goal of Creation

The sixth day is not the climax of creation. It is the penultimate. The ultimate goal of creation is discovered on the seventh day. The seventh day gives accent to *rest* and to *holiness*. God rests on the sabbath and consecrates His rest and promises participation in this goal for His creation. The biblical concept of sabbath rest involves far more than a respite from labor. It points to the end of man's *restlessness.* Where there is anxiety, there is no rest. Where there is sin, there is anxiety. If the vertical relationship between man and God is not healed, there is no sabbath. The rest and the holy are inseparable. Man is created as the image-bearer of God. Whatever else this involves, it certainly includes that man is given the privilege and the responsibility to mirror and reflect the glory and holiness of God. When this task is violated by sin, when the goal of holiness is not reached, the result is restlessness. This is the result of devastating intrusion of chaos in our lives. In sin, people are violated and anxiety becomes the order of the day. Our sin makes us "underachievers" who are doomed (apart from Christ) to spend our days in everlasting restlessness as we seek to achieve and succeed to make up for our failure to be fully the image of God. The debtor who cannot pay constantly seeks fortune, but his ship never comes in. St. Augustine began his *Confessions* with the statement, "O God, thou hast made us for thyself, and our hearts are restless until they find their rest in thee." Here, Augustine gets to the heart of the matter. Man in creation bears the mark of Cain, the sense of wandering, of lostness, until his root relationship to his Creator is restored. The Westminster Catechism begins with the question, "What is man's chief end?" The answer reads: "Man's chief end is to glorify God and to enjoy Him forever." Here, the connection between glorifying God and joy is clear. When, in disobedience, we dishonor God and "fall short of His glory," we experience restlessness. Joy is tied to obedience. The pursuit of happiness becomes the pursuit of the will-of-the-wisp if the chase is a retreat from obedience to God.

The great folly of man is in thinking that happiness is to be found outside of paradise. The wisdom of Jesus was in His understanding of the purpose of creation. He fulfilled the image of God. His meat and drink was to do the will of the Father. His command was to

". . . seek first His kingdom and His righteousness; and all these things shall be added to you" (Matt. 6:33). Jesus of Nazareth was a happy man.

The Holiness of God and the Dignity of Man

Man's dignity is rooted in the holiness of God. His dignity is derived and dependent. His dignity is a reflection of God's dignity. When man seeks dignity in himself, he succumbs to the primordial temptation, "You shall be as Gods," and exchanges his dignity for arrogance. Man, being not satisfied with the status of the highest of God's creatures, despises his dignity and, in his lust for power, loses the dignity he has. Created man is not satisfied with freedom; he searches for autonomy, and finds slavery. Man is man and he cannot be God. Somehow man hasn't learned that. Here is where Christ stands in sharp contrast with the rest of humanity. Christ was the one who ". . . did not regard equality with God a thing to be grasped, but emptied Himself, taking the form of a bondservant and being made in the likeness of men" (Phil. 2:6–7). The first Adam was not satisfied with being in the likeness of God. He grasped arrogantly for equality with God. The second Adam humbly gave up equality with God and chose to be in the likeness of man!

Herbert Richardson shows us the relationship of God's holiness to His dignity. He says:

> The *kabod* (glory) is not His nature, or essence; it does not define what God is. Nor is God's *kabod* His very existence, for the word *kabod* cannot be used as a proper name. Rather, God's *kabod* is the weightiness, heaviness, degree, or dignity proper to His being who He is. . . . Holiness refers neither to essence (i.e., to an attribute of God's nature) nor to existence (i.e., to God's very being); rather it is a *dignity*.[2]

---

[2]Herbert Richardson, *Toward an American Theology* (New York: Harper, 1967), pp. 123–24.

In this schema, the holiness of God is not seen as one attribute among many, but has reference to the totality of who God is. Thus, when we speak of God's holiness, or glory, we are dealing with God's *dignity.*

The word "dignity" is difficult to define. Yet it is, on an existential level, a very meaningful word. Many rocks have been thrown, and marches made, in our day, over the issue of human dignity. We grasp something of its meaning, but clear definitions are rare. Again, Richardson is helpful:

> Dignity is the basis of authority. It gives weight to words, i.e., turns them into commands.
> Dignity is the basis of tragedy. It is what gives life importance and redeems it from triviality.
> Dignity is the basis of meaning. It is not identical with meaning. . . . Even though life may have meaning, it may not have dignity.[3]

Here, dignity is tied in with value and worth. A number of years ago, the city of Boston was the battleground for mobsters. More than thirty gangland killings took place within a short period of time. The citizens of the town took notice of these murders, but there was no vociferous public protest about it. Then an attorney was "tail piped" and severely maimed. At once the outcry began. The public shock over the attempted murder of a law-abiding citizen was far greater than the complaint over a war between criminals. Who of us can ever forget where we were or what we were doing when we heard the initial reports of the shooting of President Kennedy? It is known as a day of infamy. The nation was outraged by an act that was described by the press as diabolical, demonic, inhuman, etc. The nation vowed never to forget this event. What used to be Idlewild International Airport is now Kennedy International Airport. What used to be Cape Canaveral is now Cape Kennedy. Countless schools, highways,

---

[3]Ibid., p. 123.

buildings, etc., all over the western world have been named in memory and honor of John F. Kennedy. Yet, on the same day, in the same city where Kennedy was killed, another man, a police officer, was killed, allegedly by the same assassin. Yet few people even remember Officer Tippet's name. Why? Was his life of less intrinsic worth or value than Kennedy's? Why don't we have a Tippet International Airport? The answer to these questions is fairly obvious. Kennedy's person was all tied up with his office, with his exalted position. He was the President of the United States. He had the dignity of his office. When a president is killed, it is not called murder, but assassination. We have a distinction of dignity built into our vocabulary. Because of the ingredients of *authority, tragedy,* and *meaning,* Kennedy's murder was a gross and heinous crime.

People do not build monuments to germs. Few people are upset when a fly is destroyed. Martin Luther King did not give his life to a movement to grant equal civil rights to black germs. The issue was the dignity of man, which is pure nonsense apart from creation. At the gut level, in the blood stream of human experience, man assumes the dignity that is ours in creation. We cannot go a city block in any major city of the Western world without finding some symbol commemorating the death of Christ. The sign of the cross is everywhere. Not one second ticks on the clock where there is not a group of people somewhere in the world gathered together at a table eating a meal ". . . in remembrance of" Him. The world cannot forget the dignity of Christ. In Him, the goal of creation is manifested. He becomes the standard of human dignity. In Him, the relationship of holiness and dignity is clearly seen. John wrote, "We beheld His glory" (John 1:14).

The "How" of Creation

One of the most stormy issues in the last century has centered on the question of the "how" of creation.

Various scientific theories have been postulated. None can be finally demonstrated, as they involve questions of early history that transcend the boundaries of empirical verification. Certain philosophical questions have also been raised. The philosophical alternatives include: one, the world is self-created; two, the world is self-existent; or, three, the world is created by something or someone other than itself, which is self-existent.

The first alternative may be reduced to logical absurdity. For the world to be self-created presupposes the world exists, which is nonsense. For something to create itself, it has to be there before it is there. The second alternative raises serious scientific questions. To posit that the universe is self-existent is to posit that the universe is eternal. Some theories do take such a position, but with enormous scientific problems. More scientific questions are raised by these theories than are solved. The third alternative is that the universe is created by something or someone who is eternal and has the power of existence in himself. One thing is absolutely certain. If something exists now, then something always existed. There must be something or someone who is eternal. To dispute this is to retreat to the absurdity of the first alternative. The issue is not whether something is eternal, but the question is, What is it that is eternal?

The biblical faith does not give a scientific description of the origin of the universe, but it does give an answer to the *who* of creation. The *how* is given in theological terms. God calls the world into existence *ex nihilo* (out of nothing). The Bible describes creation in terms of the awesome power of God's voice. He commands (by divine imperative or fiat) the world to be, and it is. The power of God's authority is graphically displayed in Christ's dealing with the dead Lazarus. When Jesus comes to the tomb, Lazarus has been dead four days. The succinct report of Lazarus' condition at that time was "He stinketh!" According to John's account, Jesus did not enter the tomb and administer artificial respiration or mouth-to-mouth resuscitation. He ordered Lazarus back to life. We are told, "He cried out with a loud voice, 'Lazarus, come forth'" (John 11:43). With that, the dead man arose. Paul says of God, ". . . who gives life to the dead and calls into being that which does not exist" (Rom. 4:17). The biblical language points to the *call* of God as the manifestation of His authority over all creation. This is not a belief in spontaneous generation, but in spontaneous creation. The Scriptures aren't interested in vain speculation about these things. Augustine's reply to the Greeks who asked, "What was God doing before He created the world?" is classic. Augustine said, "He was creating hell for curious souls!" Our confession of faith in God's act of creation is not a flight into the absurd, but is an expression of confidence in God's self-revelation. It is an affirmation that life is meaningful and that human dignity is not a maudlin fantasy.

The Relationship of the Creator to the Creation

The question of God's relationship to His creation has been a very difficult and controversial issue in the history of the Christian church. The pendulum has swung between the polar extremes of radical transcendence (*deism*) and radical immanence (*pantheism*). The "transcendence" of God refers to His being above and apart from His creation. Transcendence seeks to make a clear differentiation between the Creator and the creation. Radical transcendence views God as being totally isolated from the world. He exists, but His existence never touches human history save at the point of creation. God created the world, but He never involves Himself in it. He is viewed as *First Cause* or *Prime Mover*, but presently is at best a disinterested spectator of the affairs of men. One of the simplest varieties of radical transcendence can be seen in eighteenth-century deism. The deists viewed the world as a closed mechanical system that operated solely on the basis of fixed internal natural laws. God was often described as the heavenly watchmaker who made the intricate parts of the clock, wound it up, and then left it alone to operate and function as any other machine. God's only involvement in the machine is seen in the making, assembling, and ordering the parts according to His own design. In this, God "rules" or "governs" the machine by the internal laws at work within the machine itself.

Although deism developed historically as a conscious alternative to the Christian faith, the "synthesis-seekers" of the eighteenth century sought to adapt the naturalism of deism to the classical Christian faith. Thus, several varieties of naturalistic Christianity were developed. All recorded *intrusions* into history by God were expurgated interpretatively from the biblical narratives. Supernatural events, miracles, etc., were naturalized via relegating the stories to the level of primitive mythology (which, though they cannot be taken seriously as historical events, still have didactic value in an ethical or existential sense) or by explaining them away in purely natural terms. For example, the miracle of the feeding of the five thousand was not the result of the intrusion of divine power into the human sphere, but was actually an "ethical miracle." What happened was that Jesus was able to prevail on people who had enough foresight to bring substantial lunches to the occasion, to share their abundance with those who had nothing to eat. Thus, Jesus preformed a miracle of "sharing" that overcame the normal boundaries of the selfishness of men.

In radical transcendence, there is no room for a God who hears the groans of His people and *acts* to liberate them from bondage in Egypt. There is no room for talk of a personal relationship to a covenant Lord who commits Himself to a nation or to an individual.

Prayer becomes a therapeutic soliloquy. Incarnation becomes a gnostic redeemer myth. Radical transcendence removes God so far from history that, practically speaking, there is little difference between God and no God at all. Here, God is dead, at least His relationship to the world is dead and gone, and we are left with an impersonal machine as the object of our devotion.

At the other extreme are the radical immanentists who make a close identity between God and the totality of things. The simplest form of this may be seen in pantheism. Pantheism means literally that all is God. *Pan*—all; *theos*—God. Here, a leap is made from the omnipresence of God to the idea that God is the totality of the universe. The move is from the idea that God is present *in* everything to the idea that God *is* everything. Of course, it is one thing to say that I can see God manifested in the beauty of a flower and quite another to say that the flower is God, or a part of God. This distinction is not clear in crass forms of pantheism. (It is important to note at this point that many serious philosophers and theologians, especially those influenced heavily by Platonism and neo-Platonism, who have sought to define God in terms of His being the ground or "power" of all existence, have been unjustly accused of being pantheists in the crass sense. Though such accusations have not been valid, the responsibility lies partly with the thinkers' failure to distinguish clearly between their views and pantheism.)

The biblical view of God is one that forbids seeing God as being totally transcendent or totally immanent. There is a certain sense in which God must be seen as both. There is a qualitative distinction between God and the world that must be preserved to maintain the biblical understanding of God. The fundamental sin of Israel was idolatry, the worship of things rather than God. Further, the severe indictment that Paul brings against the pagan world in the opening section of his Epistle to the Romans reaches a climax with the words:

Professing to be wise, they became fools, and exchanged the glory of the incorruptible God for an image in the form of corruptible man and of birds and four-footed animals and crawling creatures. . . . For they exchanged the truth of God for a lie, *and worshiped and served the creature rather than the Creator,* who is blessed forever! (Rom. 1:22–23, 25).

The prohibitions against confusing God with the world are clear throughout Scripture. God is not the world. He stands apart from it in authority, in power, in dignity, and in His very being. However transcendent God may be, He is still passionately involved with His creation. His activity extends far beyond the limits of creative origins. Though He is not to be identified or confused with the world, He is nevertheless near to all of us. He is the Lord who keeps Israel, the God who does not slumber or sleep. He is the God in whom "we live and move and exist" (Acts 17:28). He is the God who notices the fall of the sparrow and counts the hairs on our heads. The "presence" of God is at the heart of the Judaeo–Christian faith. "Emmanuel" or "God-with-us" is our joy. The *Deus pro nobis* (God *for* us) is an integral part of our confession. The psalmist cries:

God is our refuge and strength, a very present help in trouble. . . . There is a river whose streams make glad the city of God, the holy dwelling place of the Most High. God is in the midst of her. . . . The LORD of hosts is with us; the God of Jacob is our stronghold (Ps. 46:1, 4–5, 7).

It is the presence of God that forms the basis of Israel's faith. The mission of the New Testament community is not activity *for* Christ, but is activity *with* Christ: activity carried out in the context of the promise, "Lo, I am with you always, even to the end of the age" (Matt. 28:20).

In creation God commits Himself to His world.

Creation does not result in the absence of God, but in the abiding presence of the One who is other from the world and yet the One who involves Himself intimately in the world. Thus, the Apostles' Creed does not end with a statement of God's making the world, but moves quickly to God's ultimate presence, the Incarnation, and to God's ultimate activity, redemption.

being articulated as the words mean "Jesus the Messiah."

The Jesus of History

New Testament scholarship has been deeply embroiled in the quest for the Jesus of history, both in the original "quest" of the nineteenth century and the "new quest" of the twentieth century. What is behind this scholarly search is an attempt to get behind the record of the New Testament understanding of Jesus to the real historical Jesus. Part of the quest is motivated by the fact that the New Testament documents do not give us an unbiased biography of the facts of the life of Jesus. Rather, the New Testament tells us about Jesus in the context of religious conviction. The Gospels, for example, are written not as a newspaper report, but as an unabashedly biased record, openly admitting the desire to persuade, to convert, and to win. John writes, "These things have been written that you may believe" (John 20:31). Also, the details of Jesus' life are repeatedly interwoven with clearly theological interpretations of the meaning of the details. Thus, the biblical record is seen not as normal historical reportage, but as *redemptive history.* Thus, the scholarly world has sought to get behind the redemptive historical interpretation of the life of Jesus to the real, concrete facts about Jesus that would provide a more objective account of who Jesus was and what He did.

The frustration of the earlier quest was that the Jesus who emerged from the "objective" investigations appeared strangely cloaked in the garb of the various schools of thought that were doing the investigation. The Hegelian school discovered a very "Idealistic" Jesus. The school of Ritschl found an "Ethical Teacher." The modern quest gives more serious attention to the New Testament documents than did the old quest, but the preliminary results of this school have resulted often in a suspiciously "existential hero" type of Jesus. As soon as we move beyond or, perhaps, behind the confines of the biblical record into the level of speculation, we are traveling on a road fraught with perils. This does not mean that all speculation about the historical Jesus is invalid or that the quests have not been helpful in bringing real insight into our understanding of Christ. But we must guard against unlimited license in reconstruction of the life of Jesus on the basis of our own pet theories. Sometimes we wonder if the place where demythologizing is necessary is not in the New Testament but in our own "objective" portraits of Jesus. How easily confusion can reign and how wild the speculation becomes when we learn that Jesus was "really" the center of a phallic-mushroom cult that had more to do with Freud than with the kingdom of God!

In any sober attempt to understand Jesus of Nazareth, we must begin with the recognition of the clear and present danger of our own cultic minds. No adult in the Western world can approach the question of Jesus with dispassionate objectivity. There is no hope for a *tabula rasa* view of Jesus. Our culture has been too involved with varieties of Christianity. The issues are too big; too much is at stake when we confront the New Testament claims to be coldly objective about them. Whether or not Jesus rose from the dead is a significant issue. Whether or not He now is actually the King of the universe to whom every man owes allegiance is not a matter of indifference. Whether or not Jesus brings to my life an absolute claim is not something I can intelligently ignore. To recognize the impossibility of total objectivity is not to abandon our pursuit of Christ in a spirit of despair. This recognition should, however, serve as a warning to remind us to check our conclusions against cultic subjectivism. We need a conservative approach to the matter. What I mean by "conservative" is not a reactionary defensive method born of fear, but a method of sober scientific investigation, born of caution. The study of history needs creative thinking, but not all creative thinking is valid. Genuine creativity involves the unique ability to perceive and demonstrate, via the data, the motivating forces that shape events. But scholarly creativity must not be confused with fanciful imagination. Even the greatest scholar is vulnerable to the subtle pressures of the academic world to come up with new ideas. Some of these "new ideas" can be wild and unbridled, and, consequently, do more to advance the career of the scholar than to advance the quest for accurate knowledge and understanding of history.

Myth of God Incarnate

Recently there has been an attack on the historicity of Christ that has received considerable publicity. *The Myth of God Incarnate* is a discussion by seven scholars about whether the Christian idea of incarnation has any viable place in modern culture. In one essay Michael Goulder tries to argue that the Incarnation was an idea taken over from the Samaritans. In another essay Frances Young examines non-Christian ideas of incarnation. It is significant to note that one of her conclusions is that there is no complete analogy to Christian claims about Christ in pre-Christian material. There is nothing novel about the thoughts conveyed in this book. Even its authors admit that there is "nothing new" in its main theme. It is essentially a popularization of recurrent themes in contemporary liberal theology.

More and more it is becoming apparent that the New Testament portrait of Jesus needs to be taken seriously not only as *redemptive* history, but also as redemptive *history*. To tell a story one believes in order to convince or persuade others of its truth does not disqualify the narrator as a credible witness. Biased observers are capable of reporting an event accurately. Whatever else we are dealing with in the gospel accounts, we are dealing with a record that comes to us from men who claim to be eyewitnesses. Luke says:

> Inasmuch as many have undertaken to compile an account of the things accomplished among us, just as those who from the beginning were eyewitnesses and servants of the Word have handed them down to us, it seemed fitting for me as well, having investigated everything carefully from the beginning, to write it out for you in consecutive order, most excellent Theophilus; so that you might know the exact truth about the things you have been taught (Luke 1:1–4).

Peter adds to this:

> For we did not follow cleverly devised tales when we made known to you the power and coming of our Lord Jesus Christ, but we were eyewitnesses of His majesty (2 Peter 1:16).

Paul replied to Festus' angry assault on his sanity:

> I am not out of my mind, most excellent Festus, but I utter words of sober truth. For the king knows about these matters, and I speak to him also with confidence, since I am persuaded that none of these things escaped his notice; for this has not been done in a corner (Acts 26:25–26).

Anyone knows that people claim to be eyewitnesses to events they never saw and that often the genuine eyewitness is very confused about what he did see. The law courts have discredited many alleged eyewitnesses who had a propensity to embellish the facts with fantasy. Festus considered Paul's testimony to be madness. Paul called it the sober truth. Be that as it may, however unreliable eyewitness testimony may be, it is certainly of more value than speculative hearsay. If one cannot accept the notion that the New Testament documents are inspired of God, at least it must be granted that these documents must be normative for our understanding of the Jesus of history. Whatever else the documents are, they are the primary sources of our knowledge of Jesus. To test their reliability by canons of speculative hypothesis is not so much an affront to piety as it is an affront to science. In any judicious quest for historical knowledge we must never begin with a predetermined view of what could or could not have happened. That would be to prejudge the case. To make the facts fit the theory rather than to allow the facts to determine the theory is a strange kind of science.

The New Testament portrait of Jesus is clearly astonishing. The record itself bears witness to the fact that the contemporaries of Jesus reacted to Him with astonishment. But the astonishing is not necessarily the incredible. The voluminous research into the basic historical integrity of the New Testament documents on points that can be tested by research has presented us with an overwhelming basis on which to be highly impressed with its accuracy and sobriety. The Gospel of Luke, for example, has been the object of magnanimous applause for its carefully detailed historical accuracy. Luke has been called the most trustworthy historian of antiquity.[1]

Rudolf Bultmann has conceded that one thing is surely true historically, i.e., that the early church had a profound faith in the Jesus of history. The issue is this: Is the picture of Jesus found in the New Testament a result of the creative faith of the early church, or is the faith of the early church a result of the real and accurate picture of Jesus found in the New Testament?

In summary, let me state that it is beyond the scope of this work to go into a detailed argument for the inspiration and infallibility of the Scriptures. The pur-

---

[1]See Norval Geldenhuys, *Commentary on the Gospel of Luke,* The New International Commentary on the New Testament (Grand Rapids: Eerdmans, 1951).

pose, rather, is to focus attention on the basic integrity of Scripture and the need for testing all speculative portraits of Jesus by the normative standard of the primary sources.

Jesus—The Messiah

The title "Messiah" conjures up all kinds of notions and concepts to the modern mind. The multi-faceted concept of messiah is not something limited to our day. In the atmosphere of the first-century Palestine, there were several different varieties of messianic expectancy present in the minds of the people. This was due not only to the forceful imagination of an oppressed people, but also the fact that there were different kinds of strands of messianic hope found in the Old Testament itself. Jesus Himself was constantly troubled by popular misconceptions of the messianic role, which was due in part to the multi-faceted Old Testament picture of the coming "Anointed One."

The three main strands of messianic expectancy that culminated in the work of Jesus were those of one, the Davidic King (Royal Messiah); two, the Son of Man (the apocalyptic heavenly being); and, three, the Suffering Servant of Isaiah.

The Son of David

The most popular and widely "expected" Messiah-type was that of the Davidic King. The Old Testament reign of King David had been the "Golden Age" of Israel. David excelled as a military hero and as a monarch. His military exploits extended the frontiers of the nation from Dan to Beersheba. During David's rule, Israel emerged as a major world power that enjoyed great military strength and economic prosperity. The Golden Age began to tarnish under Solomon's building program and soon turned to rust when the nation split under Jeroboam and Rehoboam. But the memory of exaltation lived on in the history of the people. Nostalgia reached a peak under the oppression of the Roman government. The people of the land looked to God for the "Son of David" who would restore the glory of Israel.

The frenzy of expectation surrounding the hope of a political Messiah was not born simply from nostalgia, but had its roots in concrete Old Testament prophecies that gave substance to such a hope. The Psalms had much to say about this matter. In the Psalms, David is seen as a king anointed by Yahweh Himself. Psalm 78 declares: "He also chose David His servant, and took him from the sheepfolds. . ." (v. 70). Yahweh not only anointed David, but gave several promises of future exaltation. These promises maintain:

> The LORD has sworn to David, a truth from which He will not turn back: "Of the fruit of your body I will set upon your throne. . ." (Ps. 132:11).

Also:

> So I will establish his descendants forever, and his throne as the days of heaven. . . . My covenant I will not violate, nor will I alter the utterance of my lips. Once I have sworn by My holiness; I will not lie to David. His descendants shall endure forever, and his throne as the sun before Me (Ps. 89:29, 34–36).

These promises were not obscure, but formed an important part of the religious liturgy of the people. In Israel's history, the hope of the restoration of David's throne was revived again and again. Amos prophesied: "In that day I will raise up the fallen booth of David. . ." (Amos 9:11). In each crisis period of Israel's history, the hope was rekindled.

The fact that Jesus was of the line of Judah (to whom the "scepter" was promised in Genesis 49:10), and that He was born in the city of David and was of David's seed, was not regarded as a mere coincidence by the writers of the New Testament. The New Testament writers clearly saw the fulfillment of the hope of a royal Messiah in the person of Jesus. This fact is clearly seen in the central place of importance that the ascension of Jesus is given in the New Testament. Jesus is the Son of David, who inaugurates the kingdom of God.

The central importance given to Jesus' role as King in the New Testament is often confused by the fact that frequently Jesus is at odds with those who had misconceptions of what His kingship involved. He consistently repudiated the efforts of the people to crown Him King. He refused the crown at the feeding of the 5,000. He replied to Pilate: "My kingship is not of this realm. . ." (John 18:36). To argue from this that Jesus totally repudiated the idea of Davidic kingship, or even to spiritualize this kingship totally, is to miss the point. Jesus was very much concerned with kingship. The substance of His teaching had to do with the coming of the kingdom of God. He instructed His disciples to pray for the coming of the kingdom on earth as well as in heaven. His presence inaugurated the kingdom in a certain sense. Jesus' hope of the kingdom was not a totally futuristic expectation, but it was something that had already begun, though it was not yet totally realized. There is an "already" and a "not yet" of Jesus' reign.

It is interesting that the last question the disciples asked their teacher before He left this earth had to do with the kingdom. We read:

> So when they had come together, they were asking Him, saying, "Lord, is it at this time you are restoring the kingdom to Israel?" (Acts 1:6).

Here, we see that the matter of political restoration was still a burning issue to His disciples. One might have expected Jesus to reply with some frustration, "Haven't you gotten the message? How many times do I have to tell you I'm not going to restore the kingdom to Israel?" That's not what He said. Rather, He replied: "It is not for you to know times or epochs which the Father has fixed by His own authority" (Acts 1:7). Actually, the issue is not centered on the question as to *whether* Jesus is going to restore the kingdom to Israel, but rather on the question as to *when* He will do it. The New Testament acknowledges that Jesus reigns now, but that this reign has not yet reached its highest culmination.

When we confess that Jesus is the Christ we include in that confession that He is King. The significance of that is often lost to the Western mind, particularly to the democrat who finds the concept of monarchy somewhat alien and even repugnant. The concept of absolute sovereign authority invested in a cosmic being is hard for us to grasp. Yet such a concept is implied in the title "Christ."

The Son of Man

Perhaps of all the titles ascribed to Jesus in the New Testament, this title is the one most fraught with confusion and misunderstanding. So often this title is set in contrast to the title, "Son of God," with the notion that "Son of God" refers to Jesus' divine nature and the title "Son of Man" refers to Jesus' human nature. It would be an oversimplification to say that the title "Son of God" has nothing to do with the deity of Christ and "Son of Man" nothing to do with the humanity of Christ. However, it would not be inaccurate to assert that the title "Son of Man" more clearly involves implications of deity than does the term "Son of God." Jesus' use of the title "Son of Man" was not born of a false sense of modesty or humility, but was clearly an identification of Himself with the Old Testament apocalyptic Messiah-figure found in Daniel.

Before analyzing the significance of the title "Son of Man," it might be helpful to see its use in the New Testament. Jesus is given many titles in the New Testament. The most frequent, of course, is the title "Christ." The second most frequent is the title "Lord."

The title "Son of Man" ranks third in terms of frequency, occurring some 84 times. What is tantalizing and odd about this is that, of the 84 references, 81 are found in the Gospels. The title is used only once in Acts, and twice in Revelation. Further analysis shows that, though the term is infrequently used by the New Testament writers when they are speaking about Jesus, they are careful to indicate the consistent use of the term by Jesus Himself. From this, we see not only that the writers were solicitous not to read their favorite titles back into the lips of Jesus, but also we gain real insight into Jesus' own self-understanding. Though "Son of Man" ranks third in overall New Testament usage of christological titles, it ranks *first* in Jesus' use of titles. That it was His favorite self-designation makes it a matter of very important study.[2]

The term "Son of Man" is given great theological significance in the Old Testament Book of Daniel as well as in the Apocryphal books of Enoch and 4 Ezra. It is also used to refer to the prophet Ezekiel in the book bearing his name. The figure of the "Son of Man" is an eschatological one. That is, He is one who will manifest Himself in the future, at the "end of time." He is a transcendent figure, a heavenly being who will "descend" to the earth to exercise the role of Judge.

In the Book of Daniel, the Son of Man appears in a vision of heaven. He is presented before the throne of the "Ancient of Days" and is given "dominion, glory and a kingdom, that all the peoples, nations, and men of every language might serve Him. His dominion is an everlasting dominion which will not pass away; and His kingdom is one which will not be destroyed" (Dan. 7:14). The presentation of the role of the Son of Man has close links with that of the Son of David. Both are involved in kingship, dominion, and power. But the

---

[2]Oscar Cullmann, *The Christology of the New Testament* (Philadelphia: Westminster, 1959), p. 182.

Son of David is an earthly figure and the Son of Man is a heavenly being.

The testimony of the New Testament to the pre-existence of Jesus is inseparably related to the "Son of Man" motif. He is the One who "has come from above." He is "sent" from the Father. There is a resounding theme of the *descension* of Christ that is the basis of His *acension*. ("No one has ascended into heaven, but He who descended from heaven, even the Son of Man," John 3:13).

It is not enough to declare that the New Testament writers confess that Jesus was a heavenly being. It was not just any kind of heavenly being like an angel or demiurge. He is cloaked in language restricted to deity alone. It is interesting to compare the graphic description of Daniel's version of the Ancient of Days with John's version and description of the Son of Man in the Book of Revelation:

Ancient of Days	*Son of Man*
I kept looking until thrones were set up, and the Ancient of Days took His seat; His vesture was like white snow, and the hair of His head like pure wool. His throne was ablaze with flames, its wheels were a burning fire. A river of fire was flowing and coming out from before Him; thousands upon thousands were attending Him, and myriads and myriads were standing before Him; the court sat, and the books were opened (Dan. 7:9-10).	And I turned to see the voice that was speaking with me. And having turned I saw seven golden lampstands; and in the middle of the lampstands one like a son of man clothed in a robe reaching to the feet, and girded across His breast with a golden girdle. And His head and His hair were white like white wool, like snow; and His eyes were like a flame of fire; and His feet were like burnished bronze, when it has been caused to glow in a furnace, and His voice was like the sound of many

waters. And in His right hand He held seven stars; and out of His mouth came a sharp two-edged sword; and His face was like the sun shining in its strength. And I looked, and I heard the voice of many angels around the throne and the living creatures and the elders; and the number of them was myriads of myriads, and thousands of thousands, saying with a loud voice, "Worthy is the Lamb that was slain to receive power and riches and wisdom and might and honor and glory and blessing" (Rev. 1:12–16; 5:11–12).

That the Son of Man was a figure of splendor and power cannot be doubted soberly. That He was deity is seen not only in the Old Testament portrait, but in Jesus' understanding as well. Jesus links the Son of Man with creation by saying: ". . . so the Son of Man is Lord even of the Sabbath" (Mark 2:28). To claim lordship over the Sabbath is to claim lordship over creation. The Sabbath was not merely a piece of Old Covenant legislation, but was a creation ordinance, given by the Lord of creation. Jesus also said: "But in order that you may know that the Son of Man has authority on earth to forgive sins. . ." (Luke 5:24). Here, Jesus claimed an authority that, to the Jew, was a privilege of God alone. The Jews did not miss the inferences of Jesus' claims. They sought to kill Him because His claims to deity came through loud and clear. The Son of Man came from heaven to judge the world. He would divide the sheep from the goats; He would

71

come on clouds of glory at the end of the age.

As important as it is to understand that Jesus' self-designation of "Son of Man" was not a declaration of simple humility, but was a bold claim indeed, we must not thereby overstate the case in the other direction and assume that the title "Son of Man" had nothing to do with Jesus' real humanity and real humiliation. The scandal of Jesus' teaching about Himself revolved around His suffering. He said: "The Son of Man is going to suffer at their hands"; "The Son of Man . . . came to give His life a ransom for many"; "The Son of Man has nowhere to lay His head" (Matt. 17:12; 20:28; 8:20). The heavenly being who came from the presence of the Ancient of Days is a being that entered fully into our humanity.

It has been argued that the apostle Paul developed a concept of Christ that was inconsistent with Jesus' own self-understanding. The fact that Paul never refers to Jesus as the Son of Man is used as evidence at this point. However, it is clear, as Oscar Cullmann has convincingly shown,[3] that Paul's christology is closely related to Jesus' elaboration of the Old Testament understanding of the Son of Man. Though Paul does not use the term, the concept runs through his thinking. This is especially evident in one of Paul's favorite expressions of Christ, i.e., "the second Adam." Remembering that the word, "Adam," means "man" it is easy to see the parallel relationship between Son of Man and Second Adam. Paul sets the Second Adam in striking contrast to the first Adam. In 1 Corinthians we read:

> For as in Adam all die, so also in Christ all shall be made alive. . . . So also it is written, "The first MAN Adam, BECAME A LIVING SOUL." The last Adam became a life-giving spirit. However, the spiritual is not first, but the natural; then the spiritual. The first man is from the earth, earthy; the second man is from

---

[3]Ibid., pp. 166ff.

> heaven. As is the earthy, so also are those who are earthy; and as is the heavenly, so also are those who are heavenly. And just as we have borne the image of the earthy, we shall also bear the image of the heavenly (15:22, 45–49).

Elsewhere Paul elaborates the contrast. The legacy of Adam is death; the legacy of Christ is life. Adam excels in disobedience; Christ excels in obedience. Adam receives the gift of life; Christ is the giver and source of life. Adam is of the earth, earthly; Christ accepted humiliation. All that Paul says of the second or "last" Adam is an accurate expression of the "Son of Man" motif. The Son of Man is the mediator and champion of the New Covenant. This title is the clearest biblical expression we have that confesses the dual nature of Jesus, the one in whom the fullness of the Godhead dwelt bodily.

The figure of the Son of Man lies behind the classical Western formulation of christology articulated at the Council of Chalcedon in A.D. 451. Christ is *vere deus* and *vere homo*—"truly God and truly man."

The Suffering Servant of Israel

That the figure of the Servant of the Lord or the "Suffering Servant" spoken of by the prophet Isaiah is normative to the New Testament understanding of the work of Christ is a matter that is beyond debate. The debate may continue to rage as to the identity of the author of the Book of Isaiah and over the question of the identity of the servant in the author's mind. Some maintain the servant referred to Israel corporately; others appeal to Cyrus and some to Isaiah himself. This debate will undoubtedly continue. But that the New Testament authors found in Jesus the ultimate fulfillment of the messianic figure of Isaiah is beyond question.

That Jesus conceived His own ministry in terms of Isaiah's prophecies is clear from His activity in the synagogue that marked the beginning of His public ministry. Jesus used Isaiah 61 to keynote His mission. Luke tells us:

> And He came to Nazareth, where He had been brought up; and as was His custom, He entered the synagogue on the Sabbath, and stood up to read. And the book of the prophet Isaiah was handed to Him. And He opened the book, and found the place where it was written, "The Spirit of the LORD is upon Me, because He anointed Me to preach the gospel to the poor. He has sent Me to proclaim release to the captives, and recovery of sight to the blind, to set free those who are downtrodden, to proclaim the favorable year of the Lord." And He closed the book, and gave it back to the attendant, and sat down; and the eyes of all in the synagogue were fixed upon Him. And He began to say to them, "Today this Scripture has been fulfilled in your hearing" (4:16–21).

What Jesus made abundantly clear with the statement, "Today this Scripture has been fulfilled in your hearing," He ratified with His ministry. He was the Anointed One who preached the good news to the poor and brought healing to the sick and liberation to the oppressed. When John the Baptist had doubts about Jesus' identity, and sent messengers to discuss the issue with Jesus, Jesus responded:

> Go and report to John what you have seen and heard: the BLIND RECEIVE SIGHT, the lame walk, the lepers are cleansed, and the deaf hear, the dead are raised up, the POOR HAVE THE GOSPEL PREACHED TO THEM. "And blessed is he who keeps from stumbling over Me" (Luke 7:22–23).

From these passages it is clear that Jesus' understanding of His mission cannot be understood simply in terms of His relationship to David or to the Son of Man. It is not by accident that Isaiah is the most frequently quoted prophet in the New Testament. Isaiah's prophecies are not limited to Jesus' passion, but are normative to His entire ministry.

Although Jesus defined His life in terms of Isaiah 61, it is the relationship of His death to Isaiah's view of the Suffering Servant that has most fully grasped the attention of the New Testament writers. To grasp the scope of this, I think it is necessary to quote at length from Isaiah 53.

> WHO has believed our message? And to whom has the arm of the LORD been revealed? For He grew up before Him like a tender shoot, and like a root out of parched ground; He has no *stately* form or majesty that we should look upon Him. Nor appearance that we should be attracted to Him. He was despised and forsaken of men, a man of sorrows, and acquainted with grief; and like one from whom men hide their face, He was despised, and we did not esteem Him.
>
> Surely our griefs He Himself bore, and our sorrows He carried; yet we ourselves esteemed Him stricken, smitten of God, and afflicted. But He was pierced through for our transgressions, He was crushed for our iniquities; the chastening for our well-being *fell* upon Him, and by His scourging we are healed. All of us like sheep have gone astray, each of us has turned to his own way; but the LORD has caused the iniquity of us all to fall on Him.
>
> He was oppressed and He was afflicted, yet He did not open His mouth; like a lamb that is led to slaughter, and like a sheep that is silent before its shearers, so He did not open His mouth. By oppression and judgment He was taken away; and as for His generation, who considered that He was cut off out of the land of the living, for the transgression of my people to whom the stroke *was due?* His grave was assigned to be with wicked men, yet with a rich man in His death; although He had done no violence, nor was there any deceit in His mouth.
>
> But the LORD was pleased to crush Him, putting *Him* to grief; if He would render Himself *as* a guilt offering, He will see *His* offspring, He will prolong

His days and the good pleasure of the LORD will prosper in His hand. As a result of the anguish of His soul, He will see *it* and be satisfied; by His knowledge the Righteous One, My Servant, will justify the many, as He will bear their iniquities. Therefore, I will allot Him a portion with the great, and He will divide the booty with the strong; because He poured out Himself to death, and was numbered with the transgressors; yet He Himself bore the sin of many, and interceded for the transgressors.

No matter how many times we read this description of Isaiah's Suffering Servant, we never cease to be astonished at its contents. It reads like an eyewitness account of the passion of Jesus. No wonder Isaiah's "Servant" was normative for the New Testament understanding of the cross. Here, the principles of corporate solidarity and imputation are clearly demonstrated. The scandal of Jesus is found in the centrality of His suffering to the way of redemption. John calls Him the Lamb of God who takes away the sin of the world. Jesus becomes the sin-bearer of the nation. This central New Testament theme has its roots in Isaiah 53. The Messiah comes not only as King, but also as Servant who receives the imputation of the iniquities of the people. Nowhere else does the *Deus pro nobis* (God for us) motif of Scripture ring so clearly. As Barth has pointed out, the servanthood of Jesus can be summarized in one Greek word, *"huper,"* which is translated "in behalf of."[4] The one dies for the many. Any interpretation of the life and work of Jesus that fails to take this aspect seriously does radical violence to the text of the New Testament.

Threefold Office

Christ's work has often been spoken of in terms of a threefold office. This tripartite work is seen in

---

[4]Karl Barth, *Church Dogmatics,* IV/1 (Edinburgh: T. & T. Clark, 1956), pp. 230ff.

Christ's activity as Prophet, Priest, and King. As Prophet, Jesus speaks to the people for God. He is the "Logos," the supreme and decisive "Word" of God. The Old Testament office of prophet reaches its ultimate fulfillment in Him. Jesus participates in both the foretelling and forthtelling roles of the Old Testament prophets, but He, Himself, is the supreme object of their prophecies. As Priest, Jesus fulfills the sacerdotal function of the Old Testament priesthood. He not only speaks to the people for God, as ultimate Prophet, but He speaks to God for the people as ultimate Priest. Not only does Jesus offer the supreme sacrifice, but He *is* the supreme sacrifice. He serves, not as a Levite, but as a priest forever after the order of Melchizedek. Thus, as Prophet, Priest, and King, Jesus fulfills the tripartic dimensions of the Old Testament messianic expectancy. The one who is Prophet, Priest, and King is also the Son of Man, the Suffering Servant, and the Son of David. One of the most amazing facets of the work of Jesus is found in His bringing together in one person and one ministry the many dimensions of Old Testament Messianism. Oscar Cullmann says of this:

> Both the "Suffering Servant" and the "Son of Man" already existed in Judaism. But Jesus' combination of precisely these two titles was something completely new. "Son of Man" represents the highest conceivable declaration of exaltation in Judaism; "Servant of the Lord" is the expression of the deepest humiliation. Even if there really was a concept of a suffering Messiah in Judaism, it cannot be proved that suffering was combined precisely with the idea of the Son of Man coming on the clouds of heaven. This is the unheard-of new act of Jesus, that he united these two apparently contradictory tasks in his self-consciousness, and that he expressed that union in his life and teaching.[5]

[5]Cullmann, *The Christology of the New Testament,* p. 161.

Perhaps the most striking New Testament illustration of the ironical conjunction of Christ's humiliation and exaltation is found in the imagery of Revelation 5. In this scene, John is given a vision into heaven for the opening of the scroll that was sealed. He hears the cry of the angel, "Who is worthy to open the book and to break its seals?" (Rev. 5:2). John reports with subdued emotions the fact that no one was found worthy enough for the task. His disappointment, however, gave way to grief and he said, "And I began to weep greatly, because no one was found worthy to open the book or to look into it" (Rev. 5:4). At that point an elder consoled him by saying, "Stop weeping; behold, the Lion that is from the tribe of Judah, the Root of David, has overcome so as to open the book and its seven seals" (Rev. 5:5). At this, there is an abrupt and marked change in the mood of the narrative. A sense of excited expectancy replaces the mood of despair as John awaits the "Lion" which is an image of highest royalty. The irony is complete when John does not see a Lion, but rather says, "And I saw between the throne (with the four living creatures) and the elders, a Lamb standing, as if slain . . . and He came, and He took *it* out of the right hand of Him who sat on the throne. . . . And they sang a new song, saying,

> Worthy art Thou to take the book, and to break its seals; for Thou wast slain, and didst purchase for God with Thy blood men from every tribe and tongue and people and nation. And Thou hast made them to be a kingdom and priests to our God; and they will reign upon the earth (Rev. 5:6–7, 9–10).

Here, the drama of the Apocalypse incorporates the response of the heavenly court to the Messiah. It is a response of doxology. In our confession, "We believe in Jesus, the Christ," we are ascribing to Jesus the highest liturgy of praise.

His Only Son, Our Lord. . . .

The Son of God

The creed speaks of Jesus as the only Son of God. The title, "Son of God," is a title the church has used again and again as an appeal to the biblical claim of the deity of Christ. The term, however, is a very complex one that presents us with various nuances and shades of meanings. Surely it is one of the richest titles given to Jesus in the New Testament. But as rich as it is, it is a title that has often been the source of much confusion.

Paul Van Buren, one of the leading "Death-of-God" theologians, has raised serious questions about the use of the title as a confession of Christ's deity. He points out that, "The title, 'Son,' according to biblical scholars was used in the Old Testament first as a designation for Israel and then as a designation for those who specially represented the people of the Covenant, such as the king or the high priest. The title implied serving obedience."[6]

Van Buren takes issue with the Hellenization of this title in the history of the church. That is, the term "Son" has been used in the Western world as a description of the nature of Jesus. In Greek categories the being of the Father is shared by the being of the Son. Therefore, if Jesus is "Son," He is of the same essence as the Father. The meaning of the title, "Son of God," was at the center of the Arian controversy that culminated in the formulation of the Nicene Creed. Here, the church confessed that Christ was "of the same substance" as the Father. That is, Jesus had a divine nature. Van Buren and other radical theologians argue that the title, "Son of God," has nothing to do with the nature of Christ, but everything to do with the function or office of Christ. "Son of God" then becomes not so

---

[6]Paul M. Van Buren, *The Secular Meaning of the Gospel* (New York: Macmillan, 1963), p. 48.

much a description of the person of Christ as it is a description of the work of Christ.

The critique of Van Buren and others of classical christological formulations cannot be dismissed lightly. There is much truth in Van Buren's analysis of the title. The Bible does not reserve the term, "Son of God," for Jesus. It is used of other men who are engaged in quite human activity. In the Hebrew mind, the description is primarily a description of obedience as well as a title of dignity. Though it is reserved for few men, it is still given to men.

Begotten of God

The problem is increased when we read the biblical statements of the "begottenness" of Jesus. We cannot isolate the title, "Son of God," from the references to the begottenness of Christ. John calls the "Word," the only begotten of the Father (John 1:14). The author of Hebrews calls Jesus the "first-born into the world" (Heb. 1:6) and the first-born of creation. To the Greek, the word "begotten" suggests biological progression. These texts have become the favorite proof texts of Mormons and Jehovah's Witnesses who argue that Jesus is a created being. The latter acknowledge that Jesus is exalted above all other creatures; indeed, Jesus even functions as the pre-existent Creator. Nevertheless, Christ may not be considered God Himself. That Jesus is "begotten" means only that He has a beginning in time. He is only a created being and is therefore not to be confused as eternal God. The subordination passages of the New Testament are also appealed to in this schema. Jesus prays to the Father and confesses, "The Father is greater than I" (John 14:28). Thus, the Trinity is denied on the basis of the sonship of Christ by this sect.

What is at issue between classical Christianity and contemporary sects is precisely the same point of debate that raged in the fourth century in the Arian controversy. Arius argued that one cannot be "begotten" and "eternal" at the same time. To this, the church replied that Christ was "eternally begotten," which has been a matter of controversy ever since.

This matter is not simply a question of doctrine or theoretical speculation. The matter presses on the central nerve of the life of the church, namely on worship. The fundamental sin of Israel was to worship a creature. This was regarded as the ultimate expression of blasphemy. This, of course, was the basis of hostility between Jesus and His contemporaries. Jesus wasn't killed because He told people to love each other. To give worship to Christ if He is less than God is to engage in the most heinous crime against the eternal One who is God. If Jesus were a creature and only a creature, then His claims made the cross too good for Him and His death less ghastly than His sin deserved.

Much of the confusion over the terms "Son of God" and "begotten" may be avoided if we seek to locate their meaning not in Greek categories of thought, but rather in its Semitic usage. The term "begotten" is used in the New Testament not as description of biological origin, but as a description of a unique relationship. When the Council of Nicea confessed that Christ was "begotten, not made," they were not retreating into an irrational morass of paradox, but were seeking to articulate this very point. The author of Hebrews labors the distinction between the Son and the angels (who also are sometimes called "sons"). He raises the question this way, "For to which of the angels did He ever say, 'THOU ART MY SON, TODAY I HAVE BEGOTTEN THEE'? And again, "I WILL BE A FATHER TO HIM, AND HE SHALL BE A SON TO ME'? And when He again brings the first-born into the world, He says, "AND LET ALL THE ANGELS OF GOD WORSHIP HIM.'" (Heb. 1:5–6).

In this passage Christ is exalted above the heavenly host with the command that He be worshiped. Further, Jesus received worship from Thomas and evidently found no conflict between this and the rigid monotheism of Israel. The Father is honored when the Son is worshiped, because the Father and the Son are one.

The Jehovah's Witnesses justify giving worship to Jesus by acknowledging that He is "a" god. When John says clearly, "The Word was God" (John 1:1), the Jehovah's Witness finds great significance in the absence of the definite article. He argues that John does not say Jesus was *the* God, but only that He was God (or "a god"). This kind of exegesis succeeds in making Jesus less than *the* God, but only at the expense of leaving us with the crassest kind of polytheism.

His "Only" Son

When the creed inserts the word "only," it is not intending to suggest that Christ alone is the Son of God. We are sons; angels are called sons, etc. Rather, the term suggests another kind of uniqueness. Others in the Scripture are called sons; Christ alone is called the "only-begotten." The word "only" suggests one of a kind. There is a qualitative difference between the relationship of Christ to the Father and that of any other creature. Here, the Semitic idiom expresses the uniqueness of Christ's person and work. In the word "only-begotten," Christ is set apart in a singular relationship to the Father. Here also, the Begotten One is not a creature created for a peculiar task, but is Very God of Very God, the second person of the Trinity who, in His incarnate labor, subordinates Himself to the Father for our sake. Again Philippians 2 is significant:

> Have this attitude in yourselves which was also in Christ Jesus, who, although He existed in the form of God, did not regard equality with God a thing to be grasped, but emptied Himself, taking the form of a bond-servant, and being made in the likeness of men. And being found in appearance as a man, He humbled Himself by becoming obedient to the point of death, even death on a cross (2:5–8).

Our Lord

In confessing Christ as Lord, the creed echoes the primary confession of faith of the apostolic church. The first "creed" was the simple statement, "Jesus is Lord." The title "Lord" is the most exalted title that is given to Jesus. In the culture contemporary with the New Testament, the title "Lord" (*Kurios*) had various usages. It was sometimes used as a mere form of polite address to a person, such as we would use the term "sir." It also was used to designate a slave owner or master. The apostle Paul refers to himself as a "slave" (*doulos*) of the "Lord" (*Kurios*), Jesus Christ. The slave lord purchased, owned, and governed his slaves. This connotation is used figuratively frequently in the New Testament.

Again the title "Lord" was given in a more exalted sense to those of imperial power and authority. The church faced a crisis when they were required to recite the formula *Kyros Kaisar* (Caesar is Lord) in giving a loyalty oath to the emperor. In this case, the imperial title was filled with a theological and religious connotation. Cullmann points out: "According to the ancient view, lordship over the world empire indicated lordship over the cosmos."[7] Hence, many Christians forfeited their lives by refusing to utter the loyalty oath. This was not out of a revolutionary spirit of civil disobedience, but out of a reluctance to render to Caesar that which did not properly belong to him. Absolute authority, dominion, and power belonged to Christ who alone reigns as cosmic Lord.

Most significant about the title "Lord" is its relationship to the Old Testament. The Greek translation (Septuagint) of the Old Testament used the term *Kurios* to translate the Hebrew word *Adonai*, which was a title for God Himself. When the Hebrew word *Yahweh*, which was the ineffable "name" of God, was

---

[7]Cullmann, *The Christology of the New Testament*, p. 199.

replaced in the liturgy of Israel with a substitute word, the word was *Adonai*. *Adonai* was the normative title of God in Israel that indicated God's absolute authority and power over the people and over the earth.[8]

In the Revised Standard Version of the Old Testament both the word *Yahweh* and the word *Adonai* are translated by the English word "Lord." To indicate which Hebrew word lies behind the English translation, a formal distinction in printing is used. When *Yahweh* is to be translated, the word is in capital letters: LORD. When *Adonai* is behind the text, the word "Lord" is printed in lower case letters: Lord. Psalm 8 begins, "O LORD, our Lord, how majestic is Thy name in all the earth. . . ." The Hebrew would be, "O *Yahweh*, our *Adonai*, how excellent. . . ." *Yahweh* is the "name" of God; *Adonai* is the "title" of God. This would be compared somewhat with the expression, President Ronald Reagan. "Ronald" is Reagan's name; "President" is his title, which indicates his role or function. Psalm 110 reads, "The LORD says to my Lord: Sit at My right hand. . . ." Here *Yahweh* speaks to *Adonai*, who is David's Lord, and seats Him at His right hand. In the New Testament, Jesus is the One who is elevated to the right hand of God and receives the title *Kurios*. This is the name that is "above every name" that is given to Jesus "that every tongue should confess that Jesus Christ is Lord" (Phil. 2:9b, 11).

Some may quibble that since the title "Lord" did have so many variant uses, not only in the Greek culture, but also in the New Testament, we can understand the title "Lord" not necessarily as a title of exaltation, but merely as the courteous address of "sir." To do so would do violence to the context of numerous "Lord" passages. Jesus does not call Himself the "Sir" of the Sabbath. The exalted nature of the title, however, can be seen not only from its contextual usage, but also

---

[8]Ibid., p. 200.

in its usage in the superlative form. When Jesus is called "Lord of Lords," there is no doubt what is meant. Here, absolute authority over all lesser authorities is clearly indicated.

That Jesus is objectively *the* Lord is a common assertion of the New Testament. He is the imperial authority of the entire creation. His authority has cosmic proportions. But the creed confesses not only that He is the Lord, but more specifically, He is *our* Lord. At the heart of the Christian faith is the personal submission of the believer to the authority of God's anointed and exalted King. To confess such a statement with the lips is easy. Jesus said, "Many will say to me on that day, 'Lord, Lord. . . '" but He will say to them, "I never knew you; DEPART FROM ME . . ." (Matt. 7:22–23). To say "Lord" and mean all that it implies cannot be done apart from the Holy Spirit.

Chapter 6

Conceived by the Holy Ghost, Born of the Virgin Mary

At this point, the creed shifts from a general titular confession of faith in Christ to a synoptic rehearsal of the main points of His life and work. The confession regarding the circumstances of His birth has been the most controversial of all. What engendered little debate in the early centuries of the church's history has become a boiling pot of polemics in the last two centuries. For some unknown reason, the Virgin Birth of Jesus has been isolated from the other miracle narratives of the New Testament to occupy a special concern.

The Virgin Birth has been rejected both by naturalists and supernaturalists, and that on a wide variety of grounds, ranging from the crass to the technical. Some of the more famous arguments against the Virgin Birth include the following:

Argument From Science

The most frequent objection to the Virgin Birth is that it involves a biological impossibility. In terms of fixed biological laws it is impossible for a woman to conceive a child without being inseminated in some way, either via sexual intercourse or artificial insemination. To have a "virgin" birth would involve a kind of spontaneous generation that is totally foreign to the laws of biology. It is also a type of alleged event that so far has not been duplicated in scientific experimentation.

This objection, of course, rests on the presupposition of a naturalistic, closed mechanical universe that operates according to absolutely fixed laws. Such a presupposition is theoretical at best and is at odds not only with theology, but also with contemporary philosophy of science and methodology. The scientific method is one that rests on induction for its theories, maxims, and laws. The judicious scientist (since David Hume's treatment on causality) speaks not of possibility and impossibility, but rather of *probability* quotients. If we investigate the phenomenon of conception and birth inductively and discover that, in the case of ten zillion human females, conception is always preceded by some kind of insemination, we have a strong case for a biological "law" that is based on a probability quotient of astronomical odds. However, until every force and every reality in the universe is exhaustively examined and known, no inductive principle can become an absolute law. Though something cannot be duplicated in a controlled laboratory experiment, that does not mean that it could never have happened. No laboratory experiment can eliminate all variables, as the variable of time is always a problem. What this means simply is that the scientist can make a judgment about the probability of the Virgin Birth, but cannot say that it is impossible. Perhaps this excursion into fine distinctions smacks of scholastic hairsplitting, but this point of distinction is a crucial one as it deals with the whole question of how we deal with the issue of a "unique event" which is, in the final analysis, a historical question, not a scientific one. The scientist explores what is happening, not what has happened. On the basis of an analysis of the present, all that can be gained in terms of knowledge of the past or future is a projected probability quotient. That the Virgin Birth is impossible is not a valid judgment; that, scientifically speaking, it is highly improbable is a valid judgment.

A common critique of the Christian faith attacks it at the point of miracles that involve *unique* events. Since a "unique" event cannot be duplicated or repeated, and runs counter to normal experience and cannot be verified empirically, it must be dismissed from the category of relevant testimony. If this principle of epistemology were to be consistently applied to the scientific enterprise, our whole system of knowledge would fall like Chicken Little's sky! For there to be knowledge of 100 cats, there must be knowledge of at least one cat. For there to be an analysis of a series of facts, there must be the acceptance of the first one, or you have a possible infinite series of unacceptable unique events. On the basis of this critical principle, individuation of any kind would be disallowed, and the taxonomy on which all science is based would disintegrate into a chaotic blurb of nonsense.

If the New Testament documents presented the Virgin Birth as a normal, commonplace event, indeed there would be more reasonable grounds for serious doubts of the integrity of the writers. Quite the contrary is the case. The narrative is dealing with an event that claims to be nothing less than unique. It occurs in an atmosphere of considerable astonishment wherein the principal characters involved are stunned with the difficulty of believing what is happening. The whole life of Christ is filled with "unique" events. That the gospel of Christ is astonishing is manifestly obvious. That it is impossible must be judged against the wider question of the whole meaning and destiny of the universe which is far more complicated than the normal processes of human reproduction.

What is strange is the isolation of the Virgin Birth from other miracles of Jesus by many Christians. The Virgin Birth is certainly consistent with the total New Testament portrait of Jesus. Why many people reject the Virgin Birth and yet affirm the resurrection of Christ and His sinlessness has always been an enigma to me. What is more unique than a sinless man? The point is, the Christian faith stands or falls with the uniqueness of Christ. To disavow an event because it is unique is unscientific. If I denied the beginning of the universe because it was unique, then I could give no reason why I am now engaged in a discussion about unique events. To say the Virgin Birth is possible is not to prove its truth, but at least it prevents a premature rejection of it on alleged grounds of impossibility.

Argument From Exegesis

There have been many attempts, especially in the traditional liberal school of theology, to argue that the New Testament does not even teach a Virgin Birth. The central point at issue is Matthew's use of Isaiah's prophecy concerning the "virgin" who "SHALL BE WITH CHILD, AND SHALL BEAR A SON, AND THEY SHALL CALL HIS NAME IMMANUEL" (Matt. 1:23). The quotation from Isaiah 7 raises a question concerning the word used for virgin. Isaiah speaks of an *alma* who will bear a child. The word *alma* is not the technical term for a virgin in Hebrew. Rather, the term *bethula* is the more precise clinical word for virginity. The term *alma* is more generally a "young woman." Hence the argument is that Isaiah and the New Testament writers never intended to teach anything more than that a young woman would have a baby.

This argument is invalid not only etymologically, but also contextually. The word *alma*, though not as precise as *bethula*, is less ambiguous than "young woman" and strongly suggests virginity. To illustrate this, let us examine three English terms: "virgin," "young woman," and "maiden." The term "virgin" is the English term that denotes sexual purity in the sense of being historically free of sexual intercourse. In modern terms, a "young woman" may or may not be sexually pure. Today it may not be taken for granted. All the term "young woman" can convey to us at this juncture of American culture is a description of gender and age. The term "maiden" is an archaic word used only infrequently in contemporary nomenclature. We usually find it only in poetry and in musical lyrics. The word "maiden," however, strongly connotes innocence and purity. It is not as explicit as "virgin," but far more suggestive of sexual purity than "young woman." This word is a better translation for *alma* than "young woman." Thus, *alma* is less precise than "virgin," but more explicit than "young woman."

More important to the debate, however, is the context of the story. The account of the Virgin Birth is not at all dependent on the term "virgin" in any sense. With or without the word, the concept of virginity is clearly taught. In the Lucan account of the Annunciation, Mary is told by the angel Gabriel that she will conceive and bear a son. Mary's reply to the announcement expresses bewilderment and surprise. She says, "How can this be, since I am a virgin?" (Luke 1:34). The response of the angel is, "The Holy Spirit will come upon you, and the power of the Most High will overshadow you; and for that reason the holy offspring shall be called the Son of God." (Luke 1:35). The context here can leave no room for doubt as to what is being said to Mary. Moments later the angel says to Mary, "For nothing will be impossible with God" (Luke 1:37). The question of "impossibility" is raised precisely because what has been announced violates the canons of probability.

Matthew's account is even more clear on this point. We read:

> Now the birth of Jesus Christ was as follows. When His mother Mary had been betrothed to Joseph, before they came together she was found to be with child by the Holy Spirit. And Joseph her husband, being a righteous man, and not wanting to disgrace her, desired to put her away secretly. But when he had considered this, behold, an angel of the Lord

90

> appeared to him in a dream, saying, "Joseph, son
> of David, do not be afraid to take Mary as your wife;
> for that which has been conceived in her is of the
> Holy Spirit." . . . And Joseph arose from his sleep,
> and did as the angel of the Lord commanded him,
> and took her as his wife, and kept her a virgin until
> she gave birth to a Son; and he called His name
> Jesus (Matt. 1:18–20, 24–25).

Here, Mary is pregnant before they "came together"
and was with child "of the Holy Spirit." This description, along with Joseph's reaction to the whole episode,
makes it clear to any sober reader what the intent of the
record is. That the Bible may be teaching mythological
nonsense at this point may be considered, but that the
teaching includes testimony to a Virgin Birth cannot
be denied. To argue that the New Testament record of
the Virgin Birth is false is one thing; to argue that it
does not teach a Virgin Birth or that the idea is an
interpolation can only be done via a radical violation of
the texts involved.

Argument From Infrequency of Mention

In the past few decades it has become unfashion-
able to deny the Virgin Birth on the basis of the sub-
tleties involved in the *alma-bethula* controversy. One
of the more modern bases for the denial is on the
grounds that the Virgin Birth is mentioned explicitly
only twice in the New Testament. If such a miracle oc-
curred, why isn't it mentioned in all the Gospels? Why
does Paul not make reference to it? On the basis of
these questions, the conclusion is reached that the
Virgin Birth was a fanciful story added to the history of
Jesus by Matthew and Luke.

Of all the objections to the Virgin Birth, this is the
most astonishing. The obvious question that must be
raised by those who confess that God is involved in the
totality of the New Testament is "How many times does
God have to say something before it is true?" But more

to the point than a question of piety is a question of academic consistency. If we apply the principle of frequency of mention to other matters of biblical record, we are left with far less than the Virgin Birth. Only Luke gives us a record of the Ascension of Jesus. Yet the whole concept of the lordship of Christ would be meaningless without the Ascension. Mark begins his Gospel with the ministry of John the Baptist. Mark says nothing about the Virgin Birth. In fact, he says nothing about the birth of Jesus at all. Perhaps we can infer from that that Mark believed Jesus just appeared *de novo* on the scene of His baptism. To carry the principle further in our exercise of *reductio ad absurdum,* we must maintain that the Virgin Birth, though mentioned only twice, is mentioned by two different writers. If that is not enough, what do we do with all the teaching that is unique to a particular writer? If Paul teaches a doctrine 100 times, but the doctrine is taught by no one else, must that doctrine be scrapped as well simply because it is the teaching of only one apostle? As a hermeneutical principle, how many times and by how many authors must a point be recorded before it is worthy to be considered as an article of the Christian faith? The argument from infrequency of mention must be regarded as arbitrary. If the Virgin Birth were denied or contradicted by other New Testament writers, then the question of frequency of mention may be relevant. Since that is not the case, the argument must be regarded as specious.

Argument From Mythological Parallelisms

Because a frequent motif found in pagan mythology, particularly in classical Greek mythology, is the sudden *de novo* birth of a god by the copulation of a deity with a human, it is argued that the Virgin Birth is "borrowed" from such a mythological atmosphere. The Virgin Birth then is seen as an intrusion into the biblical records by the heroes of Mt. Olympus or from Ovid's

Metamorphosis. This argument rests on two very shaky premises. First, it assumes too much in the way of parallelisms and overlooks the radical differences in historiography between the gospel writers and their Greek counterparts. To the Greek religious poet, it was not important to locate miracles in history. Actual historical events had no bearing on their polytheistic religion. To the Hebrew, history was crucial.[1] The fundamental thesis of Hebrew religion was that Yahweh was the Creator and Lord of history, and history is therefore the sphere of His self-revelation. To see this contrast, one need only compare the writing of either Ovid or Homer with Luke, paying attention not only to the similarities, but also to the differences.

The second faulty premise is a logical one. To argue that the Virgin Birth of the New Testament is drawn from virgin birth stories of pagans because the pagan stories came first is to fall into one of the most elementary logical fallacies, namely, the *post hoc ergo propter hoc* fallacy (after this, therefore, because of this).

Again, if we apply the principle of pagan parallelism consistently, rather than arbitrarily, then we must face other severe theological problems. As Bultmann has pointed out, pagan mythology not only included virgin birth stories, but also dying and rising gods. Thus, the Resurrection is also suspect (even though there is a long way from Vulcan and Prometheus to Jesus of Nazareth). Even more severe is the question of the existence of God. Because Plato believed in God, does that mean every subsequent theist is a Platonist? The questions can go on forever. What must be rejected is the selectivity of comparisons that involves a vast oversimplification of historical witnesses.

Other arguments against the Virgin Birth have

---

[1]Oscar Cullmann, *Salvation in History* (New York: Harper, 1967), and John Warwick Montgomery, *History and Christianity* (Downers Grove, Ill.: Inter-Varsity Press, 1964).

been raised by theologians like Emil Brunner, but have not received the widespread support of all higher critics. Certainly answering objections to the Virgin Birth cannot confirm it by way of negation. But the point of the discussion is that the historicity of the Virgin Birth must be dealt with in the wider context of the reliability and trustworthiness of the biblical witnesses and cannot be fairly judged if isolated out of that context.

The main concern of the New Testament is not the birth of a baby, but the Incarnation of God. With this point, the Christian faith stands or falls. In the birth narratives, we have the climactic appearance in history of the long-awaited redeemer of Israel. In the Incarnation, the *pleroma* occurs. That is, the "fullness of time" arrives. This fullness is not merely *a* fullness, but is *the* fullness. This is the *kairotic* moment that is pregnant with meaning; a moment that is both historical and historic. The Incarnation is the watershed not only of Western history which is measured in terms of B.C. and A.D., but of all history. Here is the point of convergence of the Old Testament prophecies, the moment when light enters the world. This now is where Yahweh "tents" with His people. This is the scandal to the supratemporal Greek, that the Word should become flesh. Thus, though the Gospel of John gives no report of the Virgin Birth, it is quite clear about what happens via the Virgin Birth. John says in his prologue:

> In the beginning was the Word, and the Word was with God, and the Word was God. . . . And the Word became flesh, and dwelt among us, and we beheld His glory, glory as of the only begotten from the Father . . . (John 1:1, 14).

Chapter 7

Suffered Under Pontius Pilate; Was Crucified, Dead, and Buried; Descended Into Hell

The confession of the suffering of Christ is at the core of classical Christianity. The passion of Jesus occupies a central place not only in the preaching and liturgy of the church, but also in the classical expressions of Western art. The *Pieta* is a frequent motif that seeks to capture the pregnant moment that dramatizes the climactic movement of the "great passion." The fact that the Apostles' Creed jumps from an affirmation of the birth of Christ to confession of His passion is not accidental. It brings the events of the death of Christ into sharp focus. This does not suggest that the life of Jesus was deemed insignificant by the early church, or that a negative evaluation was placed on the teaching of Jesus. Rather, the church assumed and understood that the death of Christ was meaningless apart from His life of active obedience. The death was the culmination and fruition of His teaching and could not be isolated from it.

It is the suffering of Christ that emerged as the scandal to both the Greek and the Jew of antiquity; yet the suffering of Christ was intrinsic to His messianic vocation. In Jesus' own self-consciousness, He expressed a certain compulsion for the task. He said the Son of Man "must" suffer many things. He set His face steadfastly toward Jerusalem. He assumed the role of the Suffering Servant of Israel who acquainted Himself with grief and entered fully into the human predicament. Jesus operated within the context of a destiny that involved "drinking the cup" that the Father set before Him.

The suffering of Jesus is not arbitrary or imaginary. The New Testament does not regard suffering as illusory. The Hebrew nation begins with the groaning of a people oppressed and follows a consistent historical pattern of agony and pathos. Yet the Old Testament Jews saw this passion not as the result of nihilistic forces, but as an integral part of their covenantal destiny. The biblical faith refuses to repudiate the reality of the tragic by consigning it to a lower stratum of being or by fleeing into a fanciful world of philosophical utopianism. Nor is there a capitulation to fatalism or rigid stoicism where one seeks a tranquilized state of imperturbability. Nor did the Jew give way to despair and a theology of hopelessness. Suffering is real, but it is not ultimate in the sense that it has the last voice in historical destiny. The consolation of Israel involves not a denial of suffering, but victory over it. In Christ, redemption from ultimate suffering is accomplished through suffering. His suffering has meaning; it has a purpose, in that His suffering is *for us*. It is because He suffers for us that the Man of Sorrows becomes the *Christus Victor*. The basis, then, of Christian hope lies in the believer's participation in the triumph of Christ. We become, as Paul expressed it, "super-conquerors" because of the suffering of Christ. The foundation of Christian joy is not found in an existential leap into dialectical courage, but in an assurance that rests on historical reality. Jesus did not say "Fear not" because He assumed the role of a cosmic good-humor man, who pats us on the back and tells us to "pack up your troubles in an old kit-bag and smile, smile, smile." There is no appeal to irrational sentimentality in the teaching of Christ. Rather, the exhortation: "Fear not," is followed by a *reason*, ". . . I have overcome the world" (John

16:33). This "overcoming" or "conquering" is accomplished via His suffering.

Under Pontius Pilate

That the name of Pilate appears in the creed is not without significance. Some have wondered why, of all the historical personages that surround Jesus, Pilate is given special consideration by the creed.

In the selection of Pilate there is no arbitrary assessment of guilt out of many principal participants such as Judas, Caiaphas, etc.[1] Rather, the creed selects Pilate because of his unique function in the historical unfolding of covenantal redemption.

Pilate represents the legal authority of the gentile world. Jesus is tried and judged "outside the camp," and He is "delivered to the Gentiles," or the heathen, for judgment. Here, we see the concurrence of secular history with the determined plan of redemptive history. Pilate acts not only as the executor of the authority and will of imperial Rome but is the executor of the redemptive plan of God. Jesus says somewhat enigmatically, "You would have no authority over Me, unless it had been given you" (John 19:11).

Was Crucified

That Jesus met His death by means of crucifixion has often been radically misunderstood within the church. The symbol of the cross has been virtually universal in Christendom. The meaning of that symbol has not been so universal. To examine the significance of crucifixion, we must go beyond the traditional explanation that Jesus had to be put to death by Roman means because the Jews did not have the right of capital punishment while under the juridical dominion of the Roman Empire. Had the Jews been free to execute,

---

[1]G. C. Berkouwer, *The Work of Christ* (Grand Rapids: Eerdmans, 1952), pp. 166ff.

it would have been necessary still that Jesus die outside the context of Israel. The meaning of the cross must be found within the framework of the redemptive history of Israel.

Paul relates the cross to the curse sanction of the Old Covenant. He writes:

> Christ redeemed us from the curse of the Law, having become a curse for us—for it is written, "CURSED IS EVERY ONE WHO HANGS ON A TREE"—in order that in Christ Jesus the blessing of Abraham might come to the Gentiles, so that we might receive the promise of the Spirit through faith (Gal. 3:13–14).

In this passage Paul alludes to Deuteronomy 21: 22–23, which reads:

> And if a man has committed a sin worthy of death, and he is put to death, and you hang him on a tree, his corpse shall not hang all night on the tree, but you shall surely bury him on the same day (for he who is hanged is accursed of God), so that you do not defile your land which the LORD your God gives you as an inheritance.

Thus, Paul relates the cross to the blessing-curse motif of the Old Covenant. The concept of curse is very strange to the westernized Christian and is often a point of confusion to the contemporary reader. The word "curse" gives rise to such images as the sinister epitaph of oil-can Harry, or the malevolent landlord who threatens to foreclose the mortgage in the "Perils of Pauline." More in fashion is the concept of the voodoo doctor in Haiti who puts a "curse" on his victim by sticking pins in the victim's replica doll. All of these images make it difficult for us to grasp the full import of the biblical concept of curse. In order to grasp fully the concept of curse, it is necessary to understand it within the context of the formal structure of the covenant. The form of the Old Covenant followed that which was common in suzerainty treaties between kings and vassals in the ancient Near East.[2] The covenant of Israel followed the Near Eastern pattern and included formulas of blessing and curse.[3] The blessing is promised to those who fulfill the stipulations of the covenant; the curse is threatened to those who violate the stipulations of the covenant. Deuteronomy 27 outlines several curses that accompany specific violations of the law ending with the general curse formula: "Cursed is he who does not confirm the words of this law by doing them" (v. 26). Likewise the blessing is promised to those who are obedient to the law:

> Now it shall be, if you will diligently obey the LORD your God, being careful to do all His commandments which I command you today, the LORD your God will set you high above all the nations of the earth. And all these blessings shall come upon you and overtake you, if you will obey the LORD your God (Deut. 28:1–2).

Thus, the Old Covenant clearly involves dual sanctions of blessing and curse.

The meaning of the curse may be understood in contrast to the meaning of blessing. To be blessed is the highest felicity of the Jew. Blessedness cannot be equated with ordinary happiness. Blessedness involves a transcendent dimension, a unique quality of happiness that is inseparably related to being in the presence of God and enjoying all the benefits that involves. This

---

[2]Such covenants included a *Preamble* that identified the king; a *Historical Prologue* that rehearsed the history of the relationship between the king and the vassal; the *Stipulations* that included the detailed obligations imposed upon the vassal; *Provision for deposit in the temple and periodic public reading;* the *list of gods as witnesses;* the *curses and blessings formula;* the *Formal Oath;* and the *Ceremony of Ratification.*

[3]See George E. Mendenhall, *Law and Covenant in Israel and the Ancient Near East* (Pittsburgh: The Biblical Colloquium, 1955) and Meredith Kline, *By Oath Consigned* (Grand Rapids: Eerdmans, 1968).

may be illustrated partially by a glance at the Hebrew Benediction:

> The LORD bless you and keep you; The LORD make His face shine on you, and be gracious to you; The LORD lift up His countenance on you, and give you peace (Num. 6:24–26).

In the benediction the elements of blessing include divine "keeping" or preservation, grace, and peace (in the fullest sense of the word). The blessing is stated in parallels in terms of the Lord making His face to shine on us and lifting His countenance on us. The presence of Yahweh in the midst of His people in terms of Tabernacle and Temple was the concrete assurance of God's blessing.

The curse is antithetical to the blessing. To be cursed is to be removed from the presence of God, to be set outside the camp, to be cut off from His benefits. The greatest terror to the Old Testament Jew was defilement whereby he would be pronounced "unclean" and driven out of the camp where the presence of God was focused. Adam and Eve suffered the curse to a degree when they were driven from the Garden of Eden. The scapegoat of the Old Testament sacrificial system was driven out of the camp into the wilderness after the sins of the nation were symbolically imputed to it by the laying on of hands. This "separation" from the presence of God was symbolized by the covenant sign of circumcision. The covenant in the Old Testament was not made. Rather it was "cut." The word "covenant" or "berith" means literally "a cutting." In the rite of circumcision, the Jews bore not only the mark of ethnic separation whereby they were separated to holiness and blessedness, but also carried the sign of the curse where, by means of the rite, they declared, "May I be cut off from the presence of God and His benefits if I fail to keep the stipulations (the law) of the covenant."

On the cross, Jesus was cursed. That is, He represented the Jewish nation of covenant breakers who were exposed to the curse and took the full measure of the curse on Himself. As the Lamb of God, the sin-bearer, He was cut off from the presence of God. On the cross Jesus entered into the experience of forsaken-ness on our behalf. The darkness and earthquake that accompanied the event suggest the withdrawal of the "light of His countenance." Thus, the anguish of Christ is not to be found primarily in the ghastly and tortuous pain of the physical method of execution, but rather it is located in the loss of the profound intimacy of re-lationship that the God-man Jesus enjoyed with God. On the cross God turned His back on Jesus and cut Him off from all blessing, from all keeping, from all grace, and from all peace. Jesus did not die in the tem-ple, but was killed *outside* the Holy City at the hands of the "unclean" Gentiles. Jesus was driven from the camp to experience the full horror of the unmitigated wrath of God. Nowhere in Scripture is the reality of God's wrath more sharply manifested than in the for-saking of His Messiah. Here, the negative sanction of circumcision was fulfilled. This is why Paul fought the Judaizers intensely. They sought to reinstitute the religious significance of circumcision to members of the New Covenant community. For the Christian to re-ceive circumcision as a religious rite was to repudiate its fulfillment on the cross and to place oneself once again under the obligation of the Old Covenant law.

The Cross as Sacrifice and Atonement

The meaning of the death of Christ cannot be exhausted by speaking in terms of satisfaction and substitution alone. The cross was a multi-faceted event. No amount of theological explication will ever totally penetrate the mystery that surrounds the cross. However, the cross was not an event so enigmatic that we can say nothing meaningful about it. It is not enough to see the cross as an eloquent sermon on love or the dramatic agony of an existential man. The New Testament gives us not only a report of the cross event, but also gives us considerable content regarding the *meaning* of the event. To ignore the New Testament content at this point is to make the cross a chameleon, at the mercy of the theological foliage of a given period in history for its color.

To avoid the flight into meaningless subjectivism and relativism that so often characterizes contemporary theology, we must seek to understand the cross in terms of the New Testament view of it. The cross is not an isolated event in history, but is inseparably related to Israel's national history and destiny. As noted in the section on the covenant curse, the New Testament writers looked at the cross primarily from the perspective of the Old Testament. To dismiss Paul's interpretation of the cross as being influenced heavily by gnostic redeemer myths is to miss the point and to fail to give serious attention to Paul's thorough-going Jewish background. From the beginning of Jesus' public ministry there is an atmosphere of relating His mission to the Old Testament sacrificial system. In John the Baptist's *Agnus Dei* we hear him refer to Jesus as the "Lamb of God who takes away the sin of the world" (John 1:29). This theme is repeated throughout the New Testament narrative and reaches its zenith in the Epistle to the Hebrews. In this document, the relationship between the priestly office of Jesus and the Levitical system of the Old Testament is given its fullest exposition. Jesus not only offers the perfect sacrifice for sins, but becomes, Himself, the sacrifice that is offered. The superior character of this sacrifice is seen in its being offered once for all. Thus, the uniqueness of the cross is seen in its being the fulfillment and culmination of the Old Testament sacrificial system. Jesus is the absolute oblation in that He lays down His life for His sheep.

This principle of atonement which is the means of

reconciliation between God and man is related most significantly to the Suffering Servant of Isaiah 53. That the New Testament community found its rationale for the cross in this Old Testament context cannot be disputed with sobriety. According to the witness of Luke, the risen Jesus, Himself, is the one who gives impetus to understanding the cross via the Old Testament. In His postresurrection appearance to the men on the road to Emmaus He said, by way of admonition:

> "O foolish men and slow of heart to believe in all that the prophets have spoken! Was it not necessary for the Christ to suffer these things and to enter into His glory?" And beginning with Moses and with all the prophets, He explained to them the things concerning Himself in all the Scriptures (Luke 24:25–27).

Here, Jesus Himself locates the source of interpretive content for understanding the cross, not in Heidegger's *Being and Time,* but in the Old Testament.

The issue in the church today centers on the integrity of this principle of hermeneutics. Are we to take seriously the New Testament portrait of Jesus as the Incarnate One acting in history to bring about cosmic redemption, or is the only meaning we can glean from the "myth" of Jesus an existential one that speaks to us subjectively in the "here and now"? This is not a mere intramural squabble between theologians but a debate that touches the vital nerve of the church. It reflects something of the classical struggle between the Temple and the Academy, between Abraham and Plato. The man-on-the-street must raise the question the theologian often neglects: "If the Jesus of history is not known accurately via the New Testament, why should we be concerned about Him at all?" The assertion of the church, if it is to be a church of integrity, must be that the New Testament understanding of the cross is not the mythical creation of the early church, but that it is the interpretation of an event offered by Christ Himself. If the biblical view is not only primitive, but fraudulent, it is too late now to reconstruct a dying Jesus that will be authentic. Without the biblical interpretation of the meaning of the cross, we are left to discover its meaning by our own subjective approach to the naked event. If that is the case, we are left with a meaningless cross and an irrelevant kerygma.

That the biblical categories of redemption are described in terms of the primitive should not surprise or disturb us. In the biblical revelation there is an intriguing conjunction of the simple and the complex. The ramifications of the Atonement are difficult enough to keep the most erudite scholar busily engaged for a lifetime. Yet the concept of a basis for human forgiveness via a life sacrifice is simple enough for a child to understand. The church must guard against falling unwittingly into the gnostic trap of making the gospel understandable only by an intellectual elite corps. Reconciliation is not limited to those who have the ability and propensity to master contemporary existential philosophy as a necessary prerequisite for understanding the meaning of Christ.

Dead and Buried

The fact that Christ suffered the reality of death is not without significance. So often the theme of the "blood" of Jesus is prominent in popular hymnody. This has been the occasion for much maudlin misunderstanding. The British folk-singer priest, John Guest, once raised the question: "If Jesus merely had scratched his finger on a nail, would that have been enough?" Guest's question was not motivated by sacrilege, but was intended to point out that a scratch produces blood, but not death. When the Scripture speaks of the blood of Christ, it speaks graphically concerning the primary image of life and death. The blood of Jesus is the pouring out of His life in the throes of death.

In biblical categories, death is ultimately related to sin. Death is the final curse of the law. The root of this is found in the context of the primordial prohibition given to man in creation:

> And the Lord God commanded the man, saying, "From any tree of the garden you may eat freely; but from the tree of the knowledge of good and evil you shall not eat, for in the day that you eat from it you shall surely die" (Gen. 2:16–17).

In this warning, the gift of life is forfeited by man's transgression. Hans Küng has aptly pointed out that the judgment of death is not given "in general," but the full penalty suggests *immediate* death. "In the day that you eat . . . you shall die." Thus the penalty for sin is immediate death. Küng writes:

> Sacred scripture sees death in connection with sin, and it presents this truth without glossing over it. Thus in sin the sinner earns for himself instantaneous death—instantaneous death in the massive Old Testament body-soul sense of the word. The sinner does "deserve to die."[4]

Thus, in the Covenant of Creation, sin is a capital offense. That God does not enact the penalty immediately is an indication of His grace and long-suffering. In the Old Covenant, God restricts capital punishment to a limited list of major offenses. This was an expression of grace. The New Testament list is even more limited. In contemporary civilization the list of capital crimes has been limited almost to the point of nonexistence. By cultural comparison with present-day standards, the Old Testament list of capital offenses seems severe. Yet in the total perspective of the Covenant of Creation, the Old Testament is a history, not of

---

[4]Hans Küng, *Justification*, (New York: Nelson, 1964), p. 149.

severity, but of continual mercy and long-suffering manifested by a benevolent God to His covenant-violating, life-forfeiting people. From time to time in biblical history, the people of God are given sober reminders of the divine prerogative of judgment as in the case of the death of Uzzah who touched the ark of the covenant, and Ananias and Sapphira who lied to the Holy Ghost.

Once we grasp the gravity of sin and its destructive power on persons and life, we may gain a better insight into the grace of God as He operates in history. Without an understanding of sin and the holiness of God, the Old Testament, as well as the cross, will remain a scandal to our understanding.

Jesus died. In death He received judgment. Here, the One who was obedient was stricken with the judgment of the disobedient. The judgment of the first Adam was transferred to the second Adam. The "life" of the second Adam was given to the descendants of the first Adam. Herein is the "sting" of death removed. G. C. Berkouwer writes that the death of a Christian is "no longer a payment for sin but is now simply a transfer from sin to eternal life."[5] In baptism, the Christian identifies with the death of Christ and vicariously participates in it. The transfer to life is not effected because Jesus bled, but because His bleeding was to death.

The burial of Jesus has far more significance than is usually accorded it in the liturgy and devotional life of the church. The burial actually becomes a radical point of departure in the general progression of the work of Christ from humiliation to exaltation. Its significance cannot be limited to being an external proof of the reality of death, or by seeing the burial of Jesus as the sanctification of the Christian practice of burying the dead. Rather, the true significance of the

---

[5]G. C. Berkouwer, *The Work of Christ*, p. 182.

burial is indicated in the conditions and circumstances surrounding it. The Lucan account of the burial reads:

> And behold, a man named Joseph, who was a member of the Council, a good and righteous man (he had not consented to their plan and action), *a man* from Arimathea, a city of the Jews, who was waiting for the kingdom of God; this man went to Pilate and asked for the body of Jesus. And he took it down and wrapped it in a linen cloth, and laid Him in a tomb cut into the rock, where no one had ever lain. And it was the preparation day, and the Sabbath was about to begin. Now the women who had come with Him out of Galilee followed after, and saw the tomb and how His body was laid. And they returned and prepared spices and perfumes. And on the Sabbath they rested according to the commandment (Luke 23:50–56).

Matthew adds to the description of Joseph of Arimathea the adjectival qualifier "rich" (Matt. 27:57). That Jesus was buried in the elegance of the rich stood in sharp contrast to the customary procedure of the disposal of the bodies of executed criminals. The body of Jesus was not dumped unceremoniously on the garbage heap outside of Jerusalem, but rather was treated with honor and respect. To the Jew, such treatment is important. Consider the Old Testament history regarding the death and burial of the patriarchs. Abraham's grave was a prime possession: Joseph's bones were carried out of Egypt into the Land of Promise; Moses, the mediator of the Old Covenant was buried secretly by Yahweh Himself. That the Messiah received a burial of dignity therefore signified the end of humiliation and the beginning of exaltation. The ignominy of forsakenness was over. On the cross Jesus commended His spirit to the care of the Father and His body was no longer subjected to degradation.

The most significant fact of the circumstances surrounding Jesus' burial is seen in the literal fulfillment of the predicted destiny of Isaiah's Suffering Servant:

> His grave was assigned to be with wicked men, yet with a rich man in His death; although He had done no violence, nor was there any deceit in His mouth (Isa. 53:9).

In the irony of fulfillment, Jesus is first of all numbered with the wicked in that He dies as a criminal in the company of criminals, yet He gains the burial of the rich which, in the context of the prophecy, is a positive rather than a negative factor.

Descended Into Hell

In many editions of the Apostles' Creed this statement is attended by an asterisk. Notations are often added to give explanation to this problematic phrase. Disagreement as to its meaning exists particularly between the classical Roman Catholic understanding of it and that of Protestantism. Both Roman Catholic and Lutheran theologians have viewed the descent of Christ into hell as a mission of victory and liberation to the captives there. The classical proof text for this view is found in 1 Peter 3:18–19:

> For Christ also died for sins once for all, *the* just for *the* unjust, in order that He might bring us to God, having been put to death in the flesh, but made alive in the spirit; in which also He went and made proclamation to the spirits *now* in prison.

Here, the "preaching to the spirits in prison" is regarded as an allusion to Christ's ministry that took place between the hour of His death and the moment of His Resurrection.

Some difficulty attends this theory inasmuch as the Petrine text is somewhat ambiguous as to the identity of the spirits in prison and even more unclear as to the time when this mission took place. The problem is heightened by the fact that other New Testament texts strongly suggest that Jesus was elsewhere during the three-day period between His death and resurrection. On the cross two statements are significant. First, Jesus says to the thief at His side, "Truly I say to you, today you shall be with Me in Paradise" (Luke 23:43). This passage, however, can be changed in terms of punctuation to read, "Truly, I say to you today, you shall be with me in paradise." The latter rendition is less likely, on grammatical grounds, than the former, though not impossible. Second, Jesus, at the moment of His death commended His spirit to the Father. Having the spirit of Jesus in the presence of the Father at the same time He is on a preaching mission to hell raises some very serious christological problems.

The theological issue at stake is, did Jesus experience the full penalty for sin, namely, punishment in hell? Calvin and others agree that Jesus did "descend into hell," but that descent took place not after death, but while Jesus was still on the cross. Here, in the experience of forsakenness the full torment of hell is cast on Jesus. In any case, the New Testament is clear that all that was necessary to secure the redemption of man, both in terms of active obedience and in punitive suffering, was fully accomplished and finished by Jesus, the Suffering Servant of Israel.

Chapter 8

On the Third Day He Rose Again From the Dead

In the twentieth century, the intellectual scandal of the gospel is the Resurrection of Christ. At the time of the death of Christ, and the early proclamation of the gospel by the primitive church, the scandal that the New Testament talks about, the intellectual stumbling block to the Greeks, which is called "foolishness," was not so much the Resurrection, as it was the Crucifixion. They could not understand this utter humiliation of the Servant of God. We seem to have been able to assimilate that doctrine in the history of the church, but in contemporary circles, the scandal now, intellectually, has become the Resurrection. In our day and time, we are living in a period of crisis concerning the Resurrection. There has never been a time when it was so thoroughly questioned and so critically analyzed within the church, as it is today.

In the twentieth century, resurrection is not taken for granted by the Christian church, least of all by the clergy and the academicians of the church. We're living in a time when Rudolf Bultmann's theology has captured the minds of many scholars:

> All our thinking today is shaped, irrevocably, by modern science. Blind acceptance of the New Testament mythology would be arbitrary. To press for its acceptance as an article of faith would be to reduce faith to works. Man's knowledge and mastery

of the world have advanced to such an extent through science and technology, that it is no longer possible for anyone seriously to hold the New Testament view of the world. In fact, there is no one who does. The miracles of the New Testament have ceased to be miraculous, and to defend their historicity by recourse to nervous disorders or hypnotic effects only serves to underline the fact. It is impossible to use electric light and the radio, and to avail ourselves of modern medical and surgical discoveries, and at the same time to believe in the New Testament world of spirits and miracles. We may think that we can manage it in our own lives, but to expect others to do it is to make the Christian faith unintelligible and unacceptable in the modern world.[1]

What Bultmann is saying is that the twentieth-century person, who is involved in the resources of science and medicine, understands the natural laws of the universe to such an extent that it is intellectually inconceivable for him to believe in a historical Resurrection. However, Bultmann still speaks of the risen Christ. He says that the Resurrection is a myth without historical foundation; it did not take place as a true event in space and time. Hence, he says in one breath that the man, Jesus Christ, is dead and remains dead, and in the next breath he speaks of God's having raised Jesus!

Part of the crisis in the twentieth century in coming to the Resurrection is a crisis of methodology, a crisis of communication. This involves the widespread practice of dialectical thinking. Dialectic refers to a tension between two polar opposites. Formerly, if theological statements were made that violated the law of contradiction, such statements would be regarded as nonsense. The dialectical method is one in which both

---

[1]Rudolf Bultmann, *Kerygma and Myth*, ed. H. W. Bartsch (New York: Harper and Row, 1961), p. 5.

polarities of the contradiction are stated at the same time. With the acceptance of this methodology, Bultmann can freely speak, existentially, about a God or about a Jesus of Nazareth who is dead and yet is alive. He can argue as fact that there is no resurrection in time and space as a real historical event, and yet still talk about the fact that God has raised Him from the dead. This is the way the Resurrection is often dealt with in the twentieth century. The Resurrection, in terms of historical reality, did not happen; it is a myth, but that does not make it unimportant. The fact that the early church propagated such mythology and proclaimed to the world and urged people to submit to such mythology *is* important; that's historical fact. The fact that people preached such "nonsense" underlines in red the *importance* that people attached to their understanding of the historical Jesus. So the myth is important only insofar as we see that myths sprang up around the person of Jesus. That means that these people in Jesus' lifetime learned something from the man Jesus and we can learn something from the man Jesus today, and that which we can learn, we call Christianity.

What needs to be developed is the significance of Resurrection, not as it relates to twentieth-century theology, but as it relates to the New Testament kerygma. The Kerygma was the basic, essential proclamation of the gospel. What was the content of the preaching of the apostles? When the apostles went out to preach, they used words and spoke in meaningful sentences with content that can be analyzed by the standard rules of grammar. They talked, in other words, not in terms of a rationalistic system, but they did talk reasonably. They didn't go to the people in Galatia and say that Jesus Christ is risen and yet is still dead! The first public proclamation of the Resurrection was made on the day of Pentecost when Peter was preaching, and said:

> Men of Israel, listen to these words: Jesus the
> Nazarene, a man attested to you by God with mir-
> acles and wonders and signs which God performed
> through Him in your midst, just as you yourselves
> know—this *Man,* delivered up by the predeter-
> mined plan and foreknowledge of God, you nailed to
> a cross by the hands of godless men and put *Him* to
> death. And God raised Him up again, putting an
> end to the agony of death, since it was impossible
> for Him to be held in its power (Acts 2:22–24).

He states a fact, he makes an assertion, and then
he gives a reason for that assertion and speaks in terms
of probability. If you look at a closed universe where,
from the very beginning, natural law rules and it is
impossible for anything to happen against the rules of
the universe, then Bultmann is right; it is manifestly
impossible for there to be a Resurrection. Peter said, on
the day of Pentecost, that this One who is so unique, in
such communion with God, so anointed by God, and of
such intrinsic holiness, could not possibly be held by
death. Here, we have a fundamental difference of
opinion as to what is possible. To the apostle, it was
impossible, irrational, and unthinkable to assume that
Jesus would stay dead. For twentieth-century man, it's
impossible for Him to be alive. In a world view that is
closed, God is taken completely out of the picture.[2] The
laws of nature, according to the New Testament, are
simply the normal way in which God operates the cosmos. But God is *always* in control, and in dominion as
Lord and Sovereign of the cosmos. The laws are His
laws. When we talk about the Resurrection, we're talking about a miracle, but a miracle is not something
that breaks an immutable law of nature. A miracle in
the New Testament sense is something extraordinary,
something so different from the normal course of af-

---

[2]See Clark Pinnock's discussion of this issue in *Biblical
Revelation* (Chicago: Moody Press, 1971), particularly his treatment of "The Fideists," pp. 38ff.

fairs that it brings one to complete attention. It is a sign to cause you to look. I know that in the twentieth century, one of the most normal things we observe is that when people die and are buried, they stay in the grave. It was also normal in the time of the New Testament. But the Resurrection of Jesus was not normal, it was extraordinary—"God has raised Him from the dead"—and that lies at the heart of the New Testament kerygma. The significance of that for the early church is that here, in the Resurrection, God vindicates Jesus as the true One. The God of Israel in the Old Testament, Yahweh, as well as the person of Jesus in the New Testament, was very much concerned with truth. Today, truth is often determined relativistically. That is why men live in the dialectic. The content or object of a person's faith is not so important as the person or subject who is believing it. In other words, believing is important; having faith is important. That's the credo of contemporary man; but that's *not* the credo of the New Testament. The New Testament emphasizes that it makes a difference as to what is the object of your faith. There have been many individuals throughout history who have claimed to be the leaders and founders of the only true religion. By way of contrast, in our pluralistic society, we say that it doesn't matter what you believe or in whom you believe, as long as it fulfills and satisfies you, as long as it works for you. But the point is, that there is only one person in history whom God has vindicated with the ultimate sign of authenticity—the resurrection from the dead. Thus, the apostle Peter points to David's words in the Old Testament:

> I have set the LORD continually before me; because He is at my right hand, I will not be shaken. Therefore my heart is glad, and my glory rejoices; my flesh also will dwell securely. For Thou wilt not abandon my soul to Sheol; neither wilt Thou allow Thy Holy One to see the pit. Thou wilt make known

114

to me the path of life; in Thy presence is fulness of joy; in Thy right hand there are pleasures forever (Ps. 16:8–11).

The Old Testament interpreters, the rabbinic scholars in the Talmud and other places, interpreted this passage in the Psalms to mean that David was speaking totally of himself. The apostle Peter says that David wasn't talking just about himself. Certainly, he talked about his soul, but the Holy One that he was referring to was not himself, but the One who was to come after him, his son and his Lord. Peter emphasized that David was dead and buried and that his sepulcher was with them then (at the time Peter was speaking). Accordingly, David could not have been referring to himself when he said that God would not let his body decay, because his bones are in his grave:

Brethren, I may confidently say to you regarding the patriarch David that he both died and was buried, and his tomb is with us to this day. And so, because he was a prophet, and knew that God had sworn to him with an oath to seat *one* of his descendants upon his throne, he looked ahead and spoke of the resurrection of the Christ, that He was neither abandoned to Hades, nor did His flesh suffer decay. This Jesus God raised up again, to which we are all witnesses (Acts 2:29–32).

Again, a little later, when Peter and John met a lame man begging for alms, Peter said to him:

"I do not possess silver and gold, but what I do have I give to you: In the name of Jesus Christ the Nazarene—walk!" And seizing him by the right hand, he raised him up; and immediately his feet and his ankles were strengthened (Acts 3:6–7).

When people gathered around and wondered what had happened, Peter said:

Let it be known to all of you, and to all the people of Israel, that by the name of Jesus Christ the

> Nazarene, whom you crucified, whom God raised
> from the dead—by this *name* this man stands here
> before you in good health (Acts 4:10).

Peter told the people, on that occasion, that it was not his power that raised the man from his crippled condition, but the power of Christ in His risen life.

In the New Testament, at the heart of the preaching of the early church, is the reality of the Resurrection of Jesus Christ. In 1 Corinthians 15, we have the greatest defense of the Resurrection that can be found in Scripture. In Corinth, there were people who, like Bultmann, wanted to dehistoricize the Resurrection. They were saying that Jesus did not really come back from the dead, it was only His memory that lived on. Paul speaks to these people saying:

> Now I make known to you, brethren, the gospel
> which I preached to you, which also you received, in
> which also you stand, by which also you are saved,
> if you hold fast the word which I preached to you,
> unless you believed in vain (1 Cor. 15:1–2).

What Paul does in the fifteenth chapter is very important for contemporary thinking. He thinks things through logically and offers to consider the implications of the possibility of Christ's not having been raised historically as a real space and time event. If that is absolutely true, Paul says, in other words, true for everyone and every instance that resurrection in and of itself is impossible, then the only logical conclusion that can be reached is the same as Bultmann's, i.e., that Christ is not risen.[3]

Now, Paul says, ". . . if Christ has not been raised, then our preaching is vain." Preaching was important

---

[3]At the heart of the issue with Bultmann is the question of the Judaeo-Christian approach to history. It is not without reason that Bultmann's approach has frequently been labeled as neoplatonic or neognostic, in that redemption is often removed from the plane of real history.

in the teaching and commands of Jesus and thus was important to the New Testament community. But if Christ is not raised, preaching is useless. Paul not only says that our preaching is in vain, but, ". . . your faith also is vain," because their faith (speaking of the Corinthians) is not just a subjective experience. Christian faith has an object and content. It indeed involves an emotional response and a favorable disposition of the heart, but it also involves the intellectual assent to historical reality, and so, as far as that aspect of it is concerned, if Christ is not risen, then their faith is in reality meaningless. It also follows, says Paul, that we are "false witnesses of God, because we witnessed against God that He raised Christ." Not only is our preaching futile, it is sinful, because we're lying when we tell people that God has raised up Jesus, if indeed that is not true.

Further, ". . . if Christ has not been raised . . . you are still in your sins." The atonement that was purportedly made for you is unacceptable to God and each person is left in the grip of his own sin, with no redeemer. Then Paul adds, ". . . those also who have fallen asleep in Christ have perished." Those who died believing in Christ are dead, and there is no hope of resurrection for them either: "If only we have hope in Christ in this life, we are of all men most to be pitied" (1 Cor. 15:13–19). Understandably, the apostle remonstrates:

> Why are we also in danger every hour? I protest, brethren, by the boasting in you, which I have in Christ Jesus our Lord, I die daily (1 Cor. 15:30–31).

If, after all I have gone through and suffered for Christ's sake, it is worthless because there is no resurrection, he is saying, then I might as well join the Epicureans with their philosophy of "eat, drink, and be merry, for tomorrow we die." If Christ isn't raised, then *death* is the true meaning of human existence.

The issue, as Paul sees it, is this: it's an "either-or" situation; so forget the dialectic! Either life is meaningful or it's not, and the only way there can be meaning is to know that there is something beyond life. If this life ends in death, then this life's ultimate reality is the grave. He is telling us that if there is no resurrection, we have no business to believe that there is any hope, or meaning, or significance to human existence whatsoever. Paul is not arguing that we should believe in the Resurrection of Christ merely because, if it were not true, life would be meaningless. His is not a negative apologetic. He merely draws out the implications that are inevitable, if the reality of resurrection is falsified. Paul leaves no middle ground between resurrection and meaninglessness.

Paul is attacking all positions between faith in the Resurrection and nihilism, but he is not saying that we should believe in spite of evidence to the contrary or from fear of meaninglessness in life.[4] "For I delivered to you as of first importance what I also received, that Christ died for our sins according to the Scriptures." He is appealing to us to see the trustworthiness of these ancient writings because they are being fulfilled to the letter. "And that He was buried, and that He was raised on the third day according to the Scriptures" (1 Cor. 15:3–4).

Don't forget that Paul was a Jew, and the people in Israel by their whole history had come to the place where they recognized the seriousness of the Scriptures; that the Scriptures were trustworthy because they had put their finger on reality time after time after time. He rose according to the Scriptures. If no other

---

[4]An interesting comparison could be drawn between Paul's treatment of the resurrection in 1 Corinthians 15, and Immanuel Kant's moral argument for the existence of God. Kant argues from a practical basis what is necessary for meaningful ethics. Paul does this implicitly, but goes beyond Kant to root his faith in history rather than practical necessity.

reason should compel us to believe in the Resurrection of Christ than this one, it should be enough. But Paul does not only appeal to the Scriptures, he appeals to empirical evidence:

> And that He appeared to Cephas, then to the twelve. After that He appeared to more than five hundred brethren at one time, most of whom remain until now, but some have fallen asleep. Then He appeared to James, then to all the apostles; and last of all, as it were to one untimely born, He appeared to me also (1 Cor. 15:5–8).

With his own eyes and ears, he saw and heard the risen Christ, as did many others. Peter says the same thing in 2 Peter 1:16, "For we did not follow cleverly devised tales when we made known to you the power and coming of our Lord Jesus Christ, but we were eyewitnesses of His majesty."

The implications of the resurrection of Christ are, consequently, that He is the first-born from the dead, the first among many brethren, that He goes before us, and that He has conquered the final enemy that threatens mankind—even death.

Paul therefore concludes in 1 Corinthians 15:58, "Therefore, my beloved brethren, be steadfast, immovable, always abounding in the work of the Lord, knowing that your toil is not *in* vain in the Lord." The certainty that Christian preaching and labor is not futile is inseparably related to the appearance in history of the resurrected Jesus. This knowledge is gained not via mystical intuition, nor by psychological wish-projection. It is gained via the testimony of authentic eyewitnesses whose credibility is of the highest caliber.

Chapter 9

He Ascended Into Heaven and Sits at the Right Hand of God

Unlike the Old Testament where several redemptive, historical events are commemorated by feast days, the New Testament does not institute such festivals. Apart from the institution of the Lord's Supper, there are no provisions established for any special feast days. However, the church has developed a tradition that has come to mark several occasions as high and holy festive days commemorating specific moments in the life of Christ. The entire Western world has been heavily influenced by the celebration of Christmas, Good Friday, and Easter. The Roman Catholic Church has also paid great attention to the observance of Pentecost and Ascension Day. However, these last two celebrations have been relatively obscure in classical Protestantism, having been submerged beneath the splendor of Christmas and Easter. This is indeed unfortunate, as the significance of the Ascension and Pentecost seem to be vastly underestimated in the contemporary Protestant community.

If traditional festivals are any barometer of the people's response to the acts of God in history, it seems that we have missed a point of cardinal importance in the biblical understanding of those acts. Admittedly, it is impossible to establish a calculus of value by which we can rate the relative importance of the events of Christ's life. We could argue forever over which event is the most important, the Incarnation, or the cross, or the Resurrection, etc. All of these events are interrelated and interdependent. Hence, the cross is meaningless without the Incarnation and incomplete without the Resurrection. However, none of the above events makes much sense without the Ascension. That is because the Ascension is not only the culmination of New Testament history but is also the focal point of much Old Testament prophecy.

The primary thread that is woven throughout the Old and New Testaments is the central theme of the kingdom of God. This kingdom concept reaches its zenith in the coronation of Jesus as the Messiah-King who will reign forever. Jesus cannot be King, He cannot be Lord, without the Ascension. Thus, the Ascension cannot be understood as an insignificant postscript to the work of Christ. It is not merely incidental; it is supremely important! The importance of Jesus' own self-consciousness may be grasped partially by the following statement:

> But these things I have spoken to you, that when their hour comes, you may remember that I told you of them. And these things I did not say to you at the beginning, because I was with you. But now I am going to Him who sent Me; and none of you asks Me, "Where are You going?" But because I have said these things to you, sorrow has filled your heart. But I tell you the truth, it is to your advantage that I go away; for if I do not go away, the Helper shall not come to you; but if I go, I will send Him to you. And He, when He comes, will convict the world concerning sin, and righteousness, and judgment; concerning sin, because they do not believe in Me; and concerning righteousness, because I go to the Father, and you no longer behold Me; and concerning judgment, because the ruler of this world has been judged (John 16:4–11).

This statement, of course, is only one of many allusions Jesus makes to His forthcoming departure. The statement is somewhat cryptic and leaves the disciples in a state of bewildered sorrow. Jesus discerns their emotional feelings and states that His departure is expedient for them. This must not be understood in a pejorative political fashion. Jesus is making a value judgment indicating that His absence will be advantageous to the disciples in that it is necessary for better things to come. That Jesus' absence is in any sense "better" than His incarnational presence has always been difficult for the church to grasp. The Christian often daydreams about how glorious it would be to know Jesus in the way His contemporaries did, to have the privilege of seeing what the Old Testament prophets dreamed of seeing. Yet the situation we presently enjoy, which includes the physical absence of Christ is, in a very real sense, a situation that is better than that which the disciples enjoyed. Whatever privileges they knew at the time of Jesus' sojourn on the earth, they were still living in the context of preascension history, which was not as glorious as the postascension situation.

Even the disciples came to the realization that the Ascension was not an occasion to foster lamentation. In the historical account of the Ascension itself, we read:

> And He led them out as far as Bethany, and He lifted up His hands and blessed them. And it came about that while He was blessing them, He parted from them. And they returned to Jerusalem with great joy, and were continually in the temple, praising God (Luke 24:50–53).

With this narrative the Gospel of Luke comes to a close. It is somewhat unexpected that the Gospel finishes on a joyous note inasmuch as it has just recorded the departure of Jesus. A certain amount of unreality often attends our reading of the New Testament. Frequently we fail to catch the significance of statements that should surprise us. While the Ascension was not a moment of lamentation or despair, it was a moment of departure, a time of separation. Compare this scene with a number of personal experiences that relate the separation from friends to the emotion of heavy sorrow. Contrast the mood of the disciples of Jesus at the time of His departure with the record of their earlier mood when He first announced that He would be going away.

Obviously something happened to the disciples between the initial announcement of Jesus and His actual departure. Whatever it was, it gave them a new insight and understanding of the Ascension. If the disciples were able to rejoice in their temporal separation from Jesus, it is obvious that they must have come to a degree of understanding of the Ascension that is extremely rare in the contemporary church.

It is clear from the New Testament that the Ascension is a pivotal event. Its importance, however, is not limited to the mere facts of the event. Rather, the significance of the Ascension must be seen in terms of its relationship to the present "session" of Christ at the right hand of God the Father and to the sending of the Holy Spirit on Pentecost.

To ascend in biblical categories is not merely to "go up." To be sure, the word "ascend" (*anabaino*) is commonly used in the New Testament in this way. It also takes on a cultic significance where people "go up" to Jerusalem and even a spiritual significance with reference to the ascent of the soul to heaven. But in connection with the work of the Messiah the word has a special, technical usage. It has to do with going up not to heaven in general, but to a specific place for a specific reason. The Ascension of Jesus is to the right hand of God the Father where He is exalted to the level of cosmic King and is given a unique position in the economy of the kingdom of God. In this respect, no one else "ascends" into heaven, not even David. (John magnifies this concept in the distinction he develops between the descent of Christ from heaven and His ascent to heaven.)[1]

The Ascension culminates in the "session." Jesus goes to the right hand of the Father. That is, He assumes the position of authority by which He governs the world. In this exalted position, Jesus is crowned King of Kings and Lord of Lords. That is, all authority on heaven and earth is put in His hands. Although in a certain sense Jesus' kingdom is not of this world, His reign certainly extends over this world. This does not separate the reign of Christ from earthly matters, but rather brings all earthly powers and authority structures into an inescapable relationship with Christ.

The Ascension as Ground Basis for Human Authority

Because Christ has ascended into heaven and assumed the status of cosmic King, the Christian is exhorted to an unusually high level of regard for earthly spheres of authority. That Paul, for example, exhorts slaves to be obedient to their masters and commands obedience to civil authorities that are obviously corrupt has been a matter of great consternation to many Christians. Peter exhorts:

> Submit yourselves for the Lord's sake to every human institution, whether to a king as the one in authority, or to governors as sent by him for the punishment of evildoers and the praise of those who do right (1 Peter 2:13–14).

This frequent admonition to submission to earthly rulers often seems inconsonant with the disciples' own behavior. Peter and John defied the Sanhedrin's prohibition to preach with their rhetorical proposition: "Whether it is right in the sight of God to give heed to

---

[1]See Johannes Schneider's treatment of this under "Baino" in Kittel, TDNT, Vol. I.

you rather than to God, you be the judge" (Acts 4:19). This whole question of civil obedience has become, in our generation, not merely a question of academic reflection, but one that touches the raw nerves of our entire society.

The principle in the New Testament is basically clear. When the command of the earthly magistrate conflicts with the command of God, the Christian not only may disobey the civil authority, he must do so. Stated another way, we can say we ought to obey the civil authority *unless* the civil authority commands us to do that which God forbids, or forbids us from doing that which God commands. The principle is relatively easy; the application of it is often considerably complicated.

Though the New Testament leaves room for civil disobedience and gives no simplistic categorical imperative for the Christian to give obedience in each and every situation, nevertheless there is a strong undercurrent of concern that Christians manifest a high sense of responsibility relative to civil obedience. Paul's exhortation to slaves to obey their masters is not an automatic sanction of slavery as a legitimate human institution. To the contrary, all the seeds of the abolition of this exploitive practice are clearly present in the New Testament.[2] But, applying the above-mentioned admonition, we can see that God has neither commanded the individual to seek freedom, nor has He prohibited him from accepting oppression or slavery. What we have is a call to participate in the humiliation of Christ and to bring honor to the exalted Christ.

Civil disobedience, whatever form it takes, is an unnecessary additive to an already complex situation of lawlessness. To be sure, Christians frequently feel they must break man-made laws. But the abundance of ad-

---

[2]See John Murray, *Principles of Conduct* (Grand Rapids: Eerdmans, 1957).

monition in the New Testament to the contrary must serve as a caution to us. The apostolic attitude seems to be: obey the civil authorities when you possibly can without betraying Christ, e.g., Peter calls us to do this for the Lord's sake! How then, we may ask, can the matter of our behavior in regard to the civil authorities have any bearing on our relationship to the Lord? The New Testament teaching at this point seems to arise out of a concern for the proper recognition and exaltation of the authority of Christ. There is a cosmic dimension of lawlessness that exists in the world. The judgment on the authorities of this world will be sharply focused on their refusal to submit to the authority of Christ. All authority may be traced indirectly to the ultimate authority that resides in the office of Christ. When the earthly ruler fails to bring his rule into conformity with Christ, he participates in the spirit of cosmic lawlessness, the spirit of Antichrist. The Christian lives in such a world and so is called to be different in principle. Unlike the earthly rulers, the Christian is to manifest a posture of obedience wherever and whenever possible (without compromising allegiance to Christ) lest he add to this general complex situation of lawlessness. By such submission the Christian not only participates in the humiliation of Christ and endures patient suffering, he also bears witness to a spirit of obedience that the authorities themselves so often lack. Thus, in such patient submission, testimony is given to the reality of the reign of Christ, inasmuch as our submission is not fostered by the intrinsic dignity of the magistrates, but by the dignity of Christ whom we are exalting by our obedience.

The right hand of God is the seat of ultimate authority. This position is occupied by the One whom God has anointed King. However, it is not only a royal position, it is also a judicial position as well. Here, Christ is installed as judge at the supreme tribunal of man. Christ sits on the throne of final judgment. Yet, paradoxically, the One who is judge is also the mediator of His people. Christ is at once judge and advocate, prosecutor and defense attorney. This dual role is graphically demonstrated in the account of the martyrdom of Stephen:

> Now when they heard this, they were cut to the quick, and they *began* gnashing their teeth at him. But being full of the Holy Spirit, he gazed intently into heaven and saw the glory of God, and Jesus standing at the right hand of God; and he said, "Behold, I see the heavens opened up and the Son of Man standing at the right hand of God." But they cried out with a loud voice, and covered their ears, and they rushed upon him with one impulse. And when they had driven him out of the city, they *began* stoning *him* (Acts 7:54–58a).

In this episode, as Stephen is in the process of being condemned by the ruling council of Israel, he has a vision of Jesus, *standing* at the right hand of God. To be seated at the right hand is to be in the position of judge. It is the advocate, the defense attorney that stands in the courtroom, not the judge. In the vision, Stephen catches a glimpse of the mediatorial work of Christ. As the Sanhedrin condemns Stephen to death, the ascended Christ rises to defend him! Thus, in ascension we receive not only an exalted King, but also One who is our ultimate mediator.

The Great High Priest

In biblical categories the ascent into heaven is not limited to the elevation of kingship. There is also the dimension of ascending and entering the Holy of Holies in the ultimate sense of priesthood. Jesus ascends not only to royalty, but also to the position of Intercessor as the Great High Priest. Thus, Christ ascends to the role of King-Priest. These offices, which were separate in the Old Covenant, are united in the New Covenant in the person of Christ.

Unlike the high priest of Israel who alone could enter the Holy of Holies, and that only once a year, Christ takes up residence in the ultimate Holy of Holies and involves Himself in a perpetual ministry of intercession. He fulfills the prophecy of the King who is also the Priest forever after the order of Melchizedek. The psalmist wrote:

> The LORD says to my Lord: "Sit at My right hand, until I make Thine enemies a footstool for Thy feet." The LORD has sworn and will not change His mind, "Thou art a priest forever according to the order of Melchizedek" (Ps. 110:1, 4).

That Jesus occupies the office of Intercessor is a matter of great consolation to the Christian. On a human level people enjoy being prayed for. It is commonplace to discover in people a greater sense of expectancy in matters of prayer when they have particular people praying for them. The historical development in the Roman Catholic church of seeking the intercession of departed saints in general and the Virgin Mary in particular may be rooted in this common desire for intercessors whose prayers manifest some degree of efficacy. The apostle James instructs us that, "The effective prayer of a righteous man can accomplish much" (James 5:16b). This is good news to us and an encouragement to prayer until we discover that we are not so righteous. Hence we commonly seek those we regard more righteous than ourselves that they would pray for us. Herein is the consolation of the Christian, that he has the efficacy of the prayers of Christ at his disposal. The author of Hebrews declares:

> Since then we have a great high priest who has passed through the heavens, Jesus the Son of God, let us hold fast our confession. For we do not have a high priest who cannot sympathize with our weaknesses, but one who has been tempted in all things as *we are, yet* without sin. Let us therefore draw

near with confidence to the throne of grace, that we may receive mercy and may find grace to help in time of need (Heb. 4:14–16).

The efficacy of the prayers of intercession of Jesus may be illustrated by the startling transformation in character of Peter in the New Testament. One is astonished by the radical change in his disposition from the time of his threefold denial to the period of his courageous leadership in the postascension situation. Our astonishment is dissipated somewhat, however, when we recall the words of Jesus to Peter:

Simon, Simon, behold, Satan has demanded *permission* to sift you like wheat; but I have prayed for you, that your faith may not fail; and you, when once you have turned again, strengthen your brothers (Luke 22:31–32).

Jesus not only offered prayers of intercession for Peter, but for all of His disciples, including those of us who live today, who are Christians as a result of the testimony and ministry of the first disciples. The record of Jesus' great high priestly prayer is found in John 17. I would strongly recommend that the reader set apart some time to give careful study to that chapter. Read it in personal terms, giving, if you will, your imagination free reign. Imagine Christ praying that prayer for you. There is a real sense in which that is exactly what He was doing.

Thus, in the Ascension the prayers of Christ are made available to every Christian. This is not an affirmation that deals simply with speculative material, but one that has great practical value for every believer.

The Sending of the Spirit

Though the church may rejoice in the Ascension of Christ insofar as it involves the exaltation of the Messiah to the level of cosmic King and Great High Priest, these aspects of the Ascension do not exhaust the riches that are related to that event. Primary to Jesus' evaluation of His departure as being expedient for the church is the consideration that it was a necessary prerequisite for the sending of the Comforter. The Paraclete or the Comforter is the Holy Spirit who descends on the church on the Day of Pentecost.

Pentecost marks another crucial redemptive historical event in Christianity. It is a new moment in history, but again, not a moment that is unrelated to what precedes it and what follows it. At Pentecost the Spirit comes on the people of God in a new way. Not that the Holy Spirit did not exist or was inoperative prior to Pentecost. The Old Testament is filled with references to the Holy Spirit. But at Pentecost a new epoch is inaugurated when the new covenant community is endowed by Christ and empowered to fulfill their missionary task.

The Holy Spirit in the Old Covenant

The Holy Spirit is made known as early in Israel's history as the creation account. When the earth was ". . . formless and void, and darkness was over the surface of the deep" (Gen. 1:2a), it was the Spirit of God that was ". . . moving over the surface of the waters" (Gen. 1:2b). Repeatedly throughout the Old Testament we hear of the creative power of the Spirit.

The Spirit is given to people in the Old Testament to empower them for their tasks. The judges are strengthened; the kings are anointed; the craftsmen of the tabernacle are gifted; the prophets speak under the influence of the Spirit. Yet, the anointing of the Spirit seems to be limited to relatively few individuals who are gifted for peculiar ministries of leadership.

Of the relationship between the work of the Holy Spirit in the Old Testament and that work in the New Testament, there are two particularly important Old Testament texts. The first is found in Numbers 11 where we find the record of the distribution of the

Spirit to the seventy elders under the authority of Moses. The people who had left Egypt began to complain about their present circumstances and they brought their complaints to Moses, the mediator of the Old Covenant. This dissension precipitated a crisis for Moses as he groaned beneath the burden his position of leadership imposed on him. In response to the agony of Moses, God commanded that Moses appoint seventy elders to help him with his burden. When the elders were properly assembled we are told:

> Then the LORD came down in the cloud and spoke to him; and He took of the Spirit who was upon him and placed *Him* upon the seventy elders. And it came about that when the Spirit rested upon them, they prophesied (Num. 11:25).

In response to this distribution of the Spirit to men other than Moses, some of the people (not aware of God's instructions) reacted with some discontent. Obviously this was viewed by some as an intrusion on Moses' sphere of authority. Joshua was particularly vocal in his protest to Moses, calling on Moses to forbid the elders from prophesying. Moses' response to Joshua is noteworthy and important to our understanding of Pentecost:

> But Moses said to him, "Are you jealous for my sake? Would that all the LORD's people were prophets, that the LORD would put His Spirit upon them!" (Num. 11:29).

Here, the explicit wish of Moses is that God would not only enlarge the company of those who were endowed with the Spirit but that that company would include the sum total of all the people of God, that the empowering of the Spirit would not be limited to a few isolated individuals.

This prayer of Moses became the substance of later prophecy as the prophet Joel declared:

> And it will come about after this that I will pour out
> My Spirit on all mankind; and your sons and
> daughters will prophesy, your old men will dream
> dreams, your young men will see visions. And even
> on the male and female servants I will pour out My
> Spirit in those days (Joel 2:28–29).

At Pentecost, the wish of Moses and the prophecy
of Joel are fulfilled. Now the Spirit is given to the whole
community, even down to the maidservants and the
menservants. The whole body of Christ is empowered
by God to fulfill the Great Commission. Power for mission is granted at Pentecost. The same Spirit that empowered Jesus for His ministry is now sent by Jesus to
His people. This was impossible before the Ascension.
In the Ascension Jesus gains the authority to establish
His church in the power of the Holy Spirit.

The last statement Jesus utters before the Ascension has to do with the mission of the church and the
power of the Holy Spirit:

> But you shall receive power when the Holy Spirit
> has come upon you; and you shall be My witnesses
> both in Jerusalem, and in all Judea and Samaria,
> and even to the remotest part of the earth" (Acts
> 1:8).

The seat at the right hand of God is no longer va-
cant. The coronation of the King of the kingdom of God
is no longer a vague hope of the future. The Ascension
happened. The King reigns—now.

Chapter 10

From Whence He Shall Come to Judge the Quick and the Dead

The events that surround the life of Jesus are pregnant with historical meaning. Indeed, His coming was in the fullness of time and all time is defined in light of His coming. So much of decisive significance took place that it is easy to fall into the trap of thinking that all God intends to do has already been done. But the New Testament does not merely record a *fait accompli*. On the contrary, the atmosphere of the New Testament reveals a strong sense of expectancy, an expectancy for God to complete what He has begun, to consummate what was inaugurated by the advent of Christ. There remains another chapter in redemptive history. There is still a future to the work of Christ. He has ascended; He has departed, but He left the world with an unequivocal promise that He would return to it. The final petition recorded in the New Testament is the plea, "Amen. Come, Lord Jesus" (Rev. 22:20).

When we direct our attention to the area of eschatology (the study of the "last things") we are moving into a theological sphere that is fraught with peril. It is one thing to interpret, reconstruct, and analyze the past; it is quite another to develop a theology of the future. The task is magnified not only because we are dealing with future time rather than past, but because we are entering a sphere where the biblical information often comes to us in a particularly difficult literary genre, namely, in apocalyptic-type literature. This type of literature is replete with highly imaginative symbolism that is frequently extraordinarily difficult to interpret. This type of writing is seen particularly in the Old Testament Books of Daniel and Ezekiel and the New Testament Book of Revelation. These visionary documents are often elusive to the most highly skilled biblical scholars. Let us then proceed with caution in our search for understanding the future of the kingdom.

To even discuss the matter of the return of Christ in sober terms is to run the risk of being associated with the most bizarre religious groups. Hope for an imminent return of Jesus has sparked a vast number of fanatical sects and fostered all kinds of frenetic behavior. The doomsday prophets appear in every generation and ours is not the first society to witness people who leave their daily routine to pitch their tent on some remote hillside to await the coming of Jesus. Because of the stigma associated with eschatological forecasts and messianic expectancy, there has resulted a woeful neglect of sober investigation into the future hope of Christianity. Reactions are often in the extreme and the mainstream churches' reaction to eschatological fanaticism seems to be no exception. Incredible as it may sound, coming from the pen of a Presbyterian clergyman, I have heard only one sermon dealing with the return of Jesus in a Presbyterian church in my life. This is odd in that not only the Apostles' Creed contains an affirmation of the return of Christ, but it is an article of faith in the classical Christian confessions of all major Protestant and Roman Catholic churches.

If we are to examine the content of the New Testament, we cannot afford the luxury of ignoring or obscuring this dimension that is a subject of overwhelming concern in that document. That the early church had a strong sense of expectancy of the return of Jesus can hardly be disputed. Whether or not that

expectancy has already been realized or is yet to be fulfilled is still a matter of debate.

Realized Eschatology

Growing out of the old quest for the historical
Jesus was the thesis that the kingdom came fully and
finally in the person of Jesus. Scholars have maintained that the eschaton arrived in the "coming" of
Jesus in the person of the Holy Spirit at Pentecost.
Others maintain that the destruction of Jerusalem at
the hands of the Romans in A.D. 70 signaled the "end of
the age." In a word, adherents of this position see the
present or future "coming" of Jesus in totally spiritual
terms where any concrete historical eschatology has
already been accomplished.

Variations of the above-mentioned theme were articulated by dialectical theologians such as Barth,
Brunner, and Althaus in the first part of the twentieth
century. All three of these men later abandoned the
thesis due in part to further analysis of the New Testament and in part to the massive work of Oscar
Cullmann in the area of redemptive history.[1]

The issue centers basically around the teaching of
Jesus on the Mount of Olives, usually called the Olivet
Discourse. In this discussion which is reported in the
three synoptic Gospels, Jesus instructs His disciples
regarding matters pertaining to the coming of the
kingdom and the future appearance of the Son of Man.
Here, Jesus functions in the role of true prophet ut-
tering predictions about the future. He predicts with
uncanny accuracy the destruction of the Jewish temple
and the expulsion of the Jews from Jerusalem. In addi-
tion to these events that took place near the end of the
first century, He also gave "signs" regarding His own
future coming and the close of the age.

---

[1]See particularly *Christ and Time* (Philadelphia: Westminster,
1964) and *Salvation in History* (New York: Harper, 1967).

The Signs of the Times

Much speculation has surrounded the so-called signs or indicators Jesus said would be precursors of His coming. These signs were given in response to the inquiry of the disciples:

> And as He was sitting on the Mount of Olives, the disciples came to Him privately, saying, "Tell us, when will these things be, and what *will be* the sign of Your coming, and of the end of the age?" (Matt. 24:3).

The question places the issue in the context of history. The query is twofold: *When* will it happen? and How will we know it is near? Jesus answers the query by giving a list of "signs" that will precede His coming. He prefaces the prophecy with the solemn warning: "See to it that no one misleads you" (Matt. 24:4), and He concludes the prophecy with a command: "For this reason you be ready too; for the Son of Man is coming at an hour when you do not think *He will*" (Matt. 24:44). Thus, the Olivet prophecy comes from the lips of Jesus in the context of both a warning and a command concerning careful vigilance.

The signs enumerated include wars, famines, earthquakes, false prophets, apostasy, astronomical wonders, violence, and immorality (as in the days of Noah) among others. The signs point to real events and catastrophic upheavals. Yet all of the above types of events are things that occur in every generation. The fact that every era witnesses wars, famines, earthquakes, etc., makes the whole business of interpreting the signs somewhat problematic.

History has not only demonstrated all of the above signs but also records the prognostications of very learned men who interpreted the signs of their own day in such a way as to have a sense of expectancy for the return of Christ in their own lifetime. For example, Luther read the catastrophic upheaval of the sixteenth-century Reformation as an indication of the radical nearness of the coming of Christ. Luther saw in the corruption of the papacy a manifestation of the Antichrist. Jonathan Edwards was excited about the significance of the Great Awakening and emergence of America as a new nation. He saw reason to believe in the nearness of the coming of Christ. Yet, both Luther and Edwards were wrong. This is significant for us in that these men were not religious quacks, but men of superlative quality as scholars. When we see that the giants of the church have been mistaken in their eschatological prognostications, we should be all the more careful in our own analysis. However, whatever else we can be sure of regarding the time of Christ's return, we can be sure of this: we are 450 years closer to it than Luther was and over 200 years closer to it than Edwards was.

Because of these errors in the past and the general ambiguity surrounding the signs Jesus mentioned, many scholars have abandoned all hope of attaching any eschatological significance to wars, earthquakes, etc. Indeed, it is dangerous to read too much into historical events, but it is equally hazardous to read too little into historical events. False alarms should not lead us into a dangerous state of eschatological lethargy. We still have before us the sober warning of Christ to take heed and the clear command to be vigilant.

But how can these oft-occurring kinds of events ever be considered signs of the return of Christ? If wars, famines, earthquakes, etc., occur repeatedly, the only way they can be eschatologically significant, i.e., function as "signs," is for them to occur in significant proportions. It is precisely because of such proportions that there has been an increased rash of eschatological forecasts in the twentieth century. It seems, moreover, that the modern-day prophets of doom have been more localized in the secular community than the religious community.

Twentieth-century man is more than familiar with the phenomenon of war, and is equally cognizant of "rumors" of war which in contemporary nomenclature may be called "cold" war. War is so much a part of our day that few consider the news of warfare to have any eschatological significance. However, the relative degree of warfare in the twentieth century is a striking historical phenomenon. Gordon Clark quotes Pitirim A. Sorokin's analysis of warfare in the twentieth century by means of calculating the war magnitude of every century:

> The results show that the first century of our era was the most peaceful of all; thirteenth century Europe was also an age of peace; and the nineteenth was a notable improvement over the two preceding. But the first quarter of the 20th century, by itself, was more warlike than any hundred years except the third century B.C. in Italy. . . ."[2]

When we come to the "signs" indicating natural disasters such as famines and earthquakes, again we are met with a barrage of grim forecasts by the secular analysts. It is the seismologists who are predicting a major earthquake along the San Andreas fault line in southern California which, if it occurs, will be the most devastating earthquake in recorded history. Others argue that World War III will not be fought over politics, but over food. Because of the radical character of the population-explosion problems facing underdeveloped nations, agriculturalists are predicting an imminent world famine. That a world food crisis commission has been established in Washington is evidence of the seriousness of the matter.

Apostasy is also mentioned as an eschatological sign. We must make a distinction between paganism and apostasy. Paganism involves unbelief outside of

---

[2]Gordon A. Clark, *A Christian View of Men and Things* (Grand Rapids: Eerdmans, 1952), p. 69.

the covenant community. Apostasy has to do with un-belief within the church. Again, apostasy is nothing new. It was a favorite pastime of Old Testament Israel. In New Testament history there is abundant evidence of apostasy even in that century. The church as early as apostolic times had to deal with the problem. Again, apostasy can be significant only if it occurs in notewor-thy proportions. Atheism has always been expected vis-à-vis the Christian church. But when was the death of God proclaimed loudly from within the church? When in the past was "Christian Atheism" propounded as a viable option within the church?

The history of the Western world has been, in many respects, a history of violence. Violence is nothing new to man. Civilizations come and go in the crucible of violence. Yet, comparatively speaking, we are living in a peculiarly violent era marked by riots, assassinations, and violent upheaval on a grand scale. It is interesting that "law and order" was a major issue in the 1968 Presidential election. But, it could be worse. . . .

Noah's day was characterized by an increase in sexual immorality. "Marrying and giving in marriage" is an idiomatic expression indicating a breakdown in the sexual and familial patterns of a culture. Sorokin was alarmed by the rise of the statistics of divorce in America when the statistics reached the level of one divorce in every four marriages in 1948. Since 1948 the rate has pushed close to 50%. There has also been a sharp statistical increase in the rate of illegitimate births and in venereal disease. The mores of public sex in terms of exploitation of sex in advertising, motion pictures, the theater, and in pornography have changed rather drastically. This changing cultural atmosphere is clearly evident to the man in the street. But, again, this is not enough evidence in itself to cause one to look for the immediate return of Christ.

None of the above-mentioned phenomena may mean anything, eschatologically. Perhaps the wars we know of now may be pop-gun affairs compared to future holocausts. Maybe the twenty-first or forty-fifth century may make our day look like the Golden Age of peace, prosperity, and morality. But we can't seriously compare our age with future ages inasmuch as we know nothing about them. But we can compare our age with the past, and such a comparison gives one reason to consider the possibility that we are in the twilight period of history.

The world clearly has a finite margin of error. That is, there is only so much room for man to play his games of war and exploitation of nature until he runs out of space and is faced with the real possibility of total self-destruction. There is a huge difference between the destructive potentiality of the bow and arrow and that of the nuclear bomb. Again, we can use the calculus of ratio comparisons to illustrate the clear and present danger nuclear warfare presents to modern man. Consider this: the gap in terms of destructive capacity between the bow and arrow and the bomb that was dropped on Hiroshima has been doubled since 1945. That is to say, the multimegaton bombs presently in the arsenals of the United States and the Soviet Union are as many more times destructive than the atomic bomb dropped on Hiroshima as that bomb was to a bow and arrow! The latest crisis, however, is not found in nuclear devices, but in biological weaponry that threatens to make nuclear weapons obsolete. So far no one has used these devices of horror. We have survived, since Hiroshima, without a nuclear bomb being used in warfare. How long will the restraint last? Ten years? Fifty years? Forever? Perhaps man has come of age and will, for once in history, refrain from using the weapons he has created. But, in all candor, I believe hope in man's continued self-restraint is a slim one. Yet, even if the weapons are unleashed, a small group of people may survive and continue the history of man for millions of years to come. Or, perhaps, we can now speculate into the future far enough to conceive of man's populating extraterrestrial bodies to escape the crisis of the earth. Again, it would be unwise to assert dogmatically that ours is the last generation or to fix a day and an hour of the eschaton. But there is enough evidence for all of us to be vigilant in these days.

The Jews as an Eschatological Sign

The phenomenon of the history of the Jewish people is remarkable enough to be given special consideration in the question of eschatological expectations. The whole business of eschatological expectation began with them in the first place as they looked for the fulfillment of the prophetic promise of the coming of the Day of the Lord. The dispensational school of Protestantism has given much attention to eschatology in general and the place of the Jews in eschatology in particular. However, one need not be a dispensationalist to take the history of the Jewish people seriously.

The Jews are mentioned explicitly in the Olivet Discourse. Jesus says, concerning them:

> For there will be great distress upon the land, and wrath to this people, and they will fall by the edge of the sword, and will be led captive into all the nations; and Jerusalem will be trampled underfoot by the Gentiles until the times of the Gentiles be fulfilled (Luke 21:23b–24).

This passage is usually understood to have reference to the destruction of Jerusalem and the expulsion of the Jews under the conquest of the Roman Titus. The Temple was destroyed, and thousands of Jews were either killed or taken captive by the Romans. The city of Jerusalem was taken over completely in A.D. 135, under Hadrian, after the Romans crushed the revolt of Bar Cochba. At this time, Imperial Roman law made it a capital offense for a Jew to set foot in Jerusalem.

Thus, from A.D. 70 to 1948, the Jews were in exile from their homeland. Although they were dispersed all over the world, they never lost their ethnic identity. This, in itself, is an incredible anthropological marvel. Jerusalem fell into gentile hands and remained in gentile hands until 1967. The Arab-Israeli war of 1967 provoked a renewed interest in eschatology because of the latter part of Luke 21:24. Jesus seemed to put a time limit on the captivity of Jerusalem by the Gentiles. "Jerusalem will be trampled underfoot by the Gentiles *until* the times of the Gentiles be fulfilled." The question that was raised by biblical scholars in 1967 was: Is this war part of the fulfillment of the prophecies of Olivet in that the old city of Jerusalem is now in the hands of the Jews? Again, only history can give us a final answer to this question. The debate still goes on as to whether contemporary Israel (as a nation) has any real continuity with biblical Israel.

The Appearance of the Antichrist

No discussion of eschatology would be complete without reference to the Antichrist. Paul warns the Thessalonian Christians not to be too hasty or premature in their expectation of the return of Christ by saying:

> Let no one in any way deceive you, for *it will not come* unless the apostasy comes first, and the man of lawlessness is revealed, the son of destruction, who opposes and exalts himself above every so-called god or object of worship, so that he takes his seat in the temple of God, displaying himself as being God. Do you not remember that while I was still with you, I was telling you these things? And you know what restrains him now, so that in his time he may be revealed. For the mystery of lawlessness is already at work; only he who now restrains *will do so* until he is taken out of the way. And then that lawless one will be revealed whom the Lord will slay with the breath of His mouth and

142

bring to an end by the appearance of His coming; *that is*, the one whose coming is in accord with the activity of Satan, with all power and signs and false wonders (2 Thess. 2:3–9).

This "man of lawlessness" has been identified by some with the "Beast" of Revelation 13, as the Antichrist who will be manifested prior to the return of Christ. The whole question of the nature, function, and identity of the Antichrist is a major theological problem in itself. The question is made more difficult by John's statement that "many antichrists" have come (1 John 2:18). Here, there is mention of a plurality of Antichrists, which gave rise to the speculation that the Antichrist will not appear as a particular individual but perhaps merely be the culmination of a peculiarly wicked institution. In the past, the Antichrist has been identified with Nero, Napoleon, Mussolini, Hitler, and a host of other notorious personages. The papacy has often been a favorite target for Protestants. Luther was quick to give that honor to the Pope. The original draft of the Westminster Confession of Faith equated the papacy with Antichrist. The Pope has always been a favorite target because of the religious and royal character of his office.

Whoever, or whatever the Antichrist is, it is clear that this role is understood in negative categories. He or it is described as being in an antithetical relationship to Christ and His kingdom. Paul's "man of lawlessness" strongly suggests a singular human being who will cause an extraordinary splash in history. Again, the call to vigilance is necessary lest the church be deceived by the metamorphic character of satanic association.

Many other matters concerning eschatology are constantly being debated. Will Jesus come before or after the Millennium (the thousand years of the reign of Christ on earth)? Will there even be a millennium? What does the Book of Revelation mean by a new heaven and new earth? What and when will the last judgment be? What is the status of people who have died in the interim between the ascension of Christ and His return? All of these questions and a host of others make the division of eschatology a science in itself that extends far beyond the scope of this book.

The purpose herein is that we take seriously the future dimension of redemptive history, that we may be vigilant and diligent in the mission of Christ for the present. Ours is obviously a day of urgency that obliges every Christian to the highest kind of fidelity to Christ.

Chapter 11

I Believe in the Holy Ghost

The Apostles' Creed echoes the trinitarian character of the Christian faith. That the Holy Spirit is regarded as a full member of the Trinity is often passed over and neglected. If one were to visit a library of a theological seminary or university, an interesting phenomenon could be easily noted. In a large library you might find thousands of volumes of theology dealing with the nature and work of God the Father. If that is so, you would probably find tens of thousands of books in the area of christology. By comparison, the limited number of volumes on pneumatology, the study of the person and work of the Holy Spirit, would be striking. A perusal of library material would hardly indicate a trinitarian religion. There is a woeful paucity of sober, serious material dealing with the person and work of God the Holy Spirit. We can only guess as to why this is the case. It is probably due in part to the subordinate role of the Holy Spirit in the economy of redemption, being "sent" by both the Father and the Son. Also, contributing to this problem is the difficulty that attends seeking concrete categories of definition for the Holy Spirit. The Spirit "blows where it listeth. . . ." One can find patterns of activity associated with the work of the Holy Spirit, but there remains an element of the intangible that makes fixed formulations concerning the Holy Ghost somewhat problematic. Abraham Kuyper wrote:

But the Holy Spirit is entirely different. Of him nothing appears in visible form; He never steps out from the intangible void. Hovering, undefined, incomprehensible, He remains a mystery. He is as the wind! We hear its sound, but cannot tell whence it cometh and whither it goeth. . . . There are, indeed, symbolic signs and appearances: a dove, tongues of fire, the sound of a mighty rushing wind, a breathing from the holy lips of Jesus, a laying on of hands, a speaking with foreign tongues. But of all this nothing remains; nothing lingers behind, not even the trace of a footprint.[1]

Thus, our study of the Holy Ghost must proceed on somewhat precarious footing. Precarious as it may be, however, it is a study well worth the venture. Our effectiveness as Christians, our strength as a church is inseparably related to our intimacy with the Spirit of God.

The Holy Spirit in the Old Testament

The Old Testament word for the "spirit" of God is the term *ruah*. Like the corresponding Greek term *pneuma*, it carries a multiplicity of nuances including "wind," "breath," and "spirit." In creation, the *ruah* or the "breath" of God is the vital principle of the world. God's breath communicates life not only to man, but to the animal kingdom as well. Thus, the Spirit of God operates in the Old Testament as the basic *life principle* of the universe. Without the Spirit, there is no life.[2]

The life that flows from the Spirit of God does not exhaust His work, generally speaking. The Spirit also communicates power in a unique way to individuals and nations as God directs Israel to her covenant des-

---

[1]Abraham Kuyper, *The Work of the Holy Spirit* (Grand Rapids: Eerdmans, 1956), p. 6.

[2]Walter Eichrodt, *Theology of the Old Testament*, Vol. II (Philadelphia: Westminster, 1961), pp. 46ff.

tiny. When the Spirit is manifested in the Old Testament, the effects wrought on the individual are often extraordinary and violent, indicating the awesome power of the Spirit. The New Testament consequently often refers to the Holy Spirit as the "Power of God." The term "power" denoted here is taken from the Greek *dunamis* from which our English word "dynamite" is derived.

In discussing the powerful effects often wrought by the Holy Ghost, Jonathan Edwards wrote:

> The things already mentioned have been attended also with the following things, viz., an extraordinary sense of the awful majesty, and greatness of God, as of a flame infinitely pure and bright, so as sometimes to overwhelm soul and body; a sense of the piercing all-seeing eye of God, so as sometimes to take away the bodily strength; and an extraordinary view of the infinite terribleness of the wrath of God, which has been strongly impressed on the mind, together with a sense of the ineffable misery of sinners that are exposed to this wrath, that has been overbearing. . . .[3]

Under the influence of the power of the Spirit of God, men in the Old Testament are known to respond with terror, with trembling, with ecstasy, with fainting, and with exaltation. The Spirit of God is not casual, but overpowering.

The Spirit endows leaders for specific tasks. As already discussed in the section on the Ascension, the Spirit operates frequently through the charismatic leadership of Israel. Special powers, talents, and gifts are given to individuals such as prophets, judges, craftsmen, etc. The distribution of endowments for ministry reaches its zenith in the anointing of the church at Pentecost.

---

[3]Jonathan Edwards, *The Works of President Edwards*, Vol. III (New York: Carter, 1879), p. 303.

The Work of the Holy Spirit
In Regeneration and Sanctification

The power of the Spirit is seen not only in the creative energy of the universe, but most significantly in the redemptive work of recreation. It is the intrusion of the Holy Ghost into the life of natural man that is the transforming power that brings new life. This action is called the work of regeneration. The term "regeneration" comes from the Greek, meaning "to bear," "to beget," or "to happen" a second time.

The classical expression of this concept is found in John's Gospel in the account of Jesus' conversation with Nicodemus (John 3). After a brief address of flattery to Jesus, Nicodemus is confronted by Jesus' words: "Truly, truly, I say to you, unless one is born again, he cannot see the kingdom of God" (John 3:3). Here, Jesus deals with the central theme of His teaching, i.e., the kingdom of God. He confronts one of the most learned and authoritative figures of Judaism with the necessity of regeneration. Regeneration is the *sine qua non* of understanding and of entering the kingdom of God. Without regeneration, Nicodemus is incapable of ever "seeing" the kingdom.

The point is elaborated when Nicodemus raises the question, "How can a man be born when he is old? He cannot enter a second time into his mother's womb and be born." Jesus replies to the comment by saying, "Truly, truly, I say to you, unless one is born of water and the Spirit, he cannot enter into the kingdom of God" (John 3:4–5). Thus, Jesus sets forth a necessary condition that must precede entrance into His kingdom. The condition here is that of being born of water and of the Spirit. What is meant by the allusion to water in this passage is open to various interpretations. But our immediate concern is with the allusion to the Spirit. Jesus offers some explanation and clarification by adding, "That which is born of the flesh is flesh; and that which is born of the Spirit is spirit. Do

not marvel that I said to you, 'You must be born again'"
(John 3:6–7). Jesus contrasts spiritual birth with
physical birth and rebukes Nicodemus for his astonishment. He adds, "Are you the teacher of Israel,
and do not understand these things?" (John 3:10).
Contained in this rebuke is the clear implication that
the concept Jesus is articulating is not a novel idea
unique with Him, but one that has its roots imbedded
in Old Testament redemptive history. Here is a premise
that is foundational to the biblical concept of conversion, that no one is born physically into the kingdom of
God. Rather, entrance to the kingdom is dependent
ultimately on the sovereign activity and work of the
Holy Spirit. This work cannot be automatically effected
by men or institutions, but by God alone.

The term regeneration is often used interchange-
ably with the biblical term "to quicken." This term is
used by Paul in his letter to the Ephesians and has the
meaning to "make alive":

> And you were dead in your trespasses and sins, in
> which you formerly walked according to the course
> of this world, according to the prince of the power
> of the air, of the spirit that is now working in the
> sons of disobedience. Among them we too all for-
> merly lived in the lusts of our flesh, indulging the
> desires of the flesh and of the mind, and were by
> nature children of wrath, even as the rest. But God,
> being rich in mercy, because of His great love with
> which He loved us, even when we were dead in our
> transgressions, made us alive together with Christ
> (by grace you have been saved), and raised us up
> with Him, and seated us with Him in the heavenly
> *places,* in Christ Jesus (Eph. 2:1–6).

Here, "quickening" or "making alive" has the effect
of radically changing a person from what he is by
natural birth.

The New Testament sees a sharp distinction between the "new" man and the old, natural man. The

spiritual state of natural man is portrayed in ghastly categories. The natural man is described as being "dead" in trespasses and sins, in bondage to sin, and naturally speaking, a child of wrath. In regeneration, the core of man's existence is changed. Under the influence of the Holy Spirit, a person becomes a new creation. He not only has a new disposition, or a new perspective; he is a new person. He still sins, but is no longer a slave to his sin, but is liberated by the Holy Spirit. Man is made alive to the things of God. That which once was repugnant to him in his spiritually torpid state, now fills him with delight. A new sense of values, a new life style, a new understanding of himself; a new life is wrought by the creative energy of the Spirit. The change is so effectual that Jesus describes it via the metaphor of birth. "Quickening" so alters the person that it is as if the person is born a second time. Regeneration is effected by the same Holy Spirit that "quickened" Jesus in His Resurrection. The power of resurrection is brought to bear on a person's life and he emerges from the grave of spiritual death.

The power of regeneration or of "quickening" is not contained within the talents or ability of men. Man cannot regenerate himself. Regeneration cannot be accomplished by human feat, or by self-manipulation of the will. A man does not "desire" to be regenerated. Regeneration is accomplished by the power of the Holy Spirit alone. A man can no more "quicken" himself than Lazarus could have raised himself from the dead. Self-creation or self-recreation is not within the power of man. Creation or recreation are effected by the "call" of God who says, "Let there be light!" or "Lazarus, come forth!"

Conversion Into Christ

The phrase "in Christ" is one of the most frequently used terms in the New Testament. A Christian is a person who is "in Christ," i.e., there is an identity or union between the believer and Christ. This union is not merely a legal, declarative situation where God "considers" us identified with Christ. Admittedly, there is that kind of declarative union operative in the Cross. But our union with Christ is not only declarative, but real and vital. In conversion we are really linked with Christ by the Holy Spirit. When the New Testament exhorts us to faith, we are told to believe in Christ; after we believe, we are said to be in Christ. However, two different words are used in the Greek, both of which are translated by the English word "in." When the New Testament speaks of being in Christ, the word *en* is generally used. When the exhortation "to believe in" is given, the word *eis* is used. The word *en* means to be *inside* of something; the word *eis* means to move *into* something. Thus, regeneration not only changes our nature but also effects a radical change in our relationship to Christ. Prior to conversion, we are "outside" of Christ. Faith brings us into and inside of Christ. In conversion we can really participate not only in the work of Christ, but in His person as well. We are in Him and He is in us as the Holy Spirit not only comes on us, but also dwells in us.

Either/Or of Regeneration

There is no such thing as a partially regenerate person. Regeneration is not a gradual process. Rather, regeneration is a spontaneous creative act of God. There may be a process of preparation preceding quickening, and a process of development following it, but the act itself is spontaneous. A person is either "alive" in Christ or he is not. His heart is either dead to the things of God or not. A person is either a Christian or he is not a Christian. There may be degrees of Christian growth and degrees of paganism, but there is a sharp line between the death and life of the spirit of man.

However sharp the line may be between spiritual

life and death, it is not always clear to us who has crossed the line and who hasn't. This is due in part to many factors. In the first place, there is a difference between conversion (using the term narrowly referring to regeneration) and the conversion "experience." That is, many people can point to the day and the hour when they became a Christian and are often suspicious of people who cannot pinpoint their conversion as precisely in point of time. However, regeneration and the awareness of regeneration are not the same thing. Regeneration is an objective act of God. The awareness of it is the subjective response of man. Not everyone is immediately and acutely aware of the moment of his regeneration. This is particularly true of people who are born and raised in the context of the church. To be sure, no one is born a Christian, and regeneration is a decisive event, but the Scripture nowhere enjoins that a person must be immediately aware of the influence of the Holy Spirit on his life. It is a treacherous thing indeed when an individual projects his or her own experience and seeks to make it normative for the entire Christian community. Great harm has been done by casting suspicion on people who have never experienced a sudden and dramatic conversion. The issue from the divine perspective is not *when* was a person converted, but rather *is* a person converted?

Another factor that makes it difficult for man to decide who is converted and who isn't is the fact that no two people begin their Christian life at the same point. For example, two pagans may live side by side. The first is skilled in the science of enlightened self-interest. He has no interest in God, but learns that certain evil practices are destructive personally and socially and consequently avoids them. Seeing that "crime doesn't pay," he restrains himself from gross external sins. For all outward appearances this man is a fine, upright citizen and may be regarded as a paragon of virtue. The other pagan, on the other hand, has lived without restraint. He has given himself to every form of evil and is enslaved by them all. He has an insatiable lust for illicit sexual relationships; he is an alcoholic, addicted to heroin, a compulsive liar, and a thief. Besides all this, he is hooked on cigarettes. The second man is then suddenly and dramatically converted to Christ. The immediate influence of the Holy Spirit in his life is evident in the liberation of the man from illicit sex, heroin, lying, stealing, and drinking. His life is radically changed and the change is apparent to all who know him. But the man, being not yet totally sanctified, still undergoes a terrible struggle with tobacco. Then one day Larry Legalist walks up to him and says, "I see you are not a Christian because you smoke." In Larry's eyes, the first man who is still a pagan renders more conformity to Christ than the second man. That is a tragedy, not only because no two Christians begin their Christian life at the same point, but also because no two Christians continue at the same level of sanctification. The point, of course, is not to minimize or relativize the seriousness of sin, but to point out that regeneration does not automatically convey sinlessness. It does give a person new life and a new direction, but it is a new birth that is only the beginning of sanctification. Thus, Christians must guard against making their particular level of sanctification the touchstone of everyone else's faith.

New Life in Christ

Regeneration brings new life. This concept is important to the teaching of Jesus. When Jesus defined His purpose in coming to the world, He said: "I came that they might have life, and might have *it* abundantly" (John 10:10).

Again, some confusion exists between the New Testament Greek and English. As the above statement comes to us in the English text, it sounds enigmatic. If Jesus came to bring life, why didn't He limit His mission to visiting the cemeteries of the world? Obviously Jesus has something more in mind than biological vitality. This can be clarified somewhat by seeing that the New Testament has two different words, both of which are translated by the English word "life." The term *bios* (from which the English word "biology" is derived) is generally used with reference to the biotic aspects of human existence, such as the normal life processes of breathing, etc. On the other hand, the term *zoa* (from which the English word "zoology" is derived) has a rather unique meaning in the teaching of Jesus. It is not a reference simply to bodily functions, but rather to a quality of life. Jesus speaks of a new dimension of existence that is qualitatively different from that to which man is accustomed. The source of this life is found in Christ Himself and He understood His mission in terms of making this new quality of existence available to us. This life is given by Christ by the power of the Holy Spirit. Without the Holy Spirit, man lacks this dimension of life offered by Christ.

Sanctification

The work of the Holy Spirit does not end with regeneration. He does not quicken a person and leave the rest of the Christian life to be lived by the intrinsic ability of the person. Regeneration is the beginning of the Christian life, but it is not the end of it. The end or the goal of the Christian life is conformity to the image of Christ. The Christian is called to mature in obedience and righteousness. This maturing process is also accomplished by the power of the Holy Spirit. The power to grow into holiness (which is what the term "sanctification" means) is initiated, sustained, and completed by the Holy Spirit. When the Holy Spirit enters the life of a believer, one of His goals is to aid the believer in becoming actually holy.

In justification, a person is counted righteous by God in view of the person's union with Christ through faith. The merit of Christ is imputed to the believer. Thus, we enter into a relationship with God, not on the basis of our own righteousness, but on the basis of the righteousness of Christ. But justification is not the end of the Christian life. Through the process of sanctification we are not just counted righteous, but are in fact, slowly becoming righteous. This process will not be completed in this life, but it certainly begins here.

After the intrusion of the Holy Spirit into a person's life, there is a sense in which, theologically speaking, the Christian becomes schizophrenic. That is, he is involved in a tremendous conflict and struggle. This struggle is described in biblical terms as a warfare between two natures. There is conflict between the natural inclination to sin that characterizes the old man and the desire to please God that characterizes the new man. There is a sense in which life is never so complicated as it is when a person becomes a Christian. Many well-meaning witnesses have pleaded the Christian faith by dramatically proclaiming something like "Come to Jesus and all your troubles will be over." That sounds appealing, but it is unmitigated nonsense. When a person becomes a Christian he knows joy and peace unspeakable, but he also knows the agony of being thrust into a struggle of almost cosmic proportions. Life takes on a new degree of seriousness and suddenly the stakes are higher. The goal of perfection is set before the Christian. This goal has caused many who failed to understand grace, to faint. We begin the struggle with the victory already guaranteed. But the campaign is filled with frequent failure and defeat. Like the apostle Paul, we do the very things we do not (touching our new nature) desire to do. The quest for obedience is not always easy and endurance is often a costly matter. But the quest is worth the struggle and endurance is worth the price. That is why the Christian can never view God's abiding grace and forgiveness as a license to sin.

Quietism and Activism

In the quest for a holy life, two extremes often manifest themselves as obstacles to sanctification. These extremes may be termed "quietism" and "activism." Quietism, as an extreme form, sees the work of sanctification as being totally the work of the Holy Spirit. In this schema, a person offers no effort or exertion toward sanctification, but rather quietly waits for the Holy Spirit to change his life. This position obviously reflects a woeful lack of understanding of the Christian's responsibility to cooperate with the Holy Ghost in sanctification. It also neglects the manifold admonitions of Christ and the apostles to exercise diligence and self-discipline in seeking holiness.

Activism is the polar opposite of quietism. In this syndrome, the person frantically seeks his sanctification on the basis of his own strength. He is constantly endeavoring to be perfect by his own ability, without any dependence on the Holy Ghost. This particular method of sanctification is doomed to failure from the outset.

There is a sense in which the Christian must be actively quiet, or quietly active in the sense that he seeks all that he can from the Holy Spirit, and gives all that he has of himself to the goal of sanctification. There is no final experience in this life that ends the struggle. A person can speak in tongues ten thousand times, and still not be free from the influence of sin in his life. He may hear heavenly voices, see ecstatic visions, have heartwarming experiences at a thousand altars, but the quest for holiness goes on. There are no easy solutions and no substitutes that can allow a person to afford the luxury of eliminating the daily disciplines of prayer, study of Scripture, fellowship, worship, service, etc.

Perhaps the reader is not a Christian and is totally bewildered by all this talk of the Holy Spirit. Maybe the Holy Spirit is an unknown reality to him. Or perhaps the reader is a model Christian mature in every way in the things of Christ. In either case, or in any case, wherever the reader may be in his understanding of Christ, I am certain that he can go deeper and deeper into the person and work of the Holy Spirit. None of us have gone beyond scratching the surface of holiness and of knowing the ineffable sweetness of communing with God the Holy Spirit. As it is written:

> THINGS WHICH EYE HAS NOT SEEN AND EAR HAS NOT HEARD, AND *which* HAVE NOT ENTERED THE HEART OF MAN, ALL THAT GOD HAS PREPARED FOR THOSE WHO LOVE HIM. For to us God revealed *them* through the Spirit; for the Spirit searches all things, even the depths of God (1 Cor. 2:9–10).

Chapter 12

The Holy Catholic Church; the Communion of Saints

There appears to be an increasing disenchantment with organized religion and the institutional church in America, particularly in the minds of the younger generation. Criticism from within and without is often the order of the day. The American church has been fragmented denominationally and polarized theologically to such a degree that it seems almost quixotic to speak of the church as being "Holy." It has been argued that the church is the most corrupt organization in the world. Such a statement can only be hyperbole. However, if any truth resides in such a charge it would be because the church is the most important organization in the world. It is corrupt for many reasons, not the least of which is that it is the target of every demonic, hostile attack in the universe. There is a biblical guarantee from the lips of Christ that the gates of hell will never prevail against the church. There is no guarantee that the gates of hell would not be unleashed against it.

From the liberal side of the theological spectrum comes the lament that the church is saddled with cumbersome, outmoded traditions that make it almost impossible for it to relate in a relevant way to the critical issues of our society. The conservative wing anguishes over the loss of the pristine purity of the New Testament church. The split between the two is not imaginary. On the surface the main line Protestant denominations have more or less moved in a direction of theological pluralism in order to allow both sides to coexist in some kind of organizational unity. However, the churches continue to be polarized over the issue of "personal evangelism" versus "social action." As a result, many local churches operate basically on a congregational level with only token involvement in higher judicatories, councils, conventions, etc.

So what do we do? Do we write off the contemporary institutional church as an unnecessary vestigial appendage from a forgotten era? Do we consider the church an anachronism that has no relevance to our age? Do we start a new denomination and add to the proliferation of splinter groups? Do we move in the direction of merger into one monolithic structure that will give organizational unity without resolving the gut-level theological issues that already exist? I wish I knew the answers to these questions. It is one thing to describe the church—it's quite another to reform it.

What seems to be agreed upon by many people on both sides of the issue is that the status quo is intolerable and that change and reformation are not optional, but necessary. But as soon as the question of change is raised it brings into sharp focus the following necessary question, i.e., change to what? In what direction should we go? That question is then answered on the basis of the divergent theological opinions already held by the dividing parties, and usually serves to heighten the issues that divide us. Thus, we are left in a vicious and ruthless dilemma where the status quo is intolerable, and change is tolerable to some and radically intolerable to others.

To determine the course of change there must first be a standard or authority on which value judgments can be made. The formal principle that lurked behind Luther's disputation on the question of justification, is the same principle that underlies our struggle today, namely, the question of authority. Luther's answer to this emerged quite clearly at the Diet of Worms in his articulation of *Sola Scriptura.* Thus, the Bible became the final court of appeal to the Reformers. Whatever else they thought about Scripture concerning inspiration, exegesis, canonicity of certain books, hermeneutics, etc., upon one thing they agreed, namely, the ruling authority of the apostolic teaching. The Reformation carried with it the cry *Ad Fontes*—to the source. The New Testament church was to be the paradigm for reconstruction.

What resulted from such a massive program of reformation is visible today. In America alone there are over two thousand Protestant denominations all claiming to be following the New Testament paradigm!

Obviously, someone is not really following the New Testament. Is the New Testament church that obscure? Obviously, there is room for differences of opinion in matters of exegesis and in areas where the New Testament is silent. But these factors alone cannot be responsible for the theological and ecclesiastical chaos that exists today. Rather, we must also include at least two more prominent contributing factors. The first is the deplorable state of biblical illiteracy that exists in the church today. The second and perhaps most important is the widespread *de facto* rejection of the Scriptures as the authority in the faith and practice of the church.

If both the authority of the church as invested in Pope and/or councils and the authority of the Scripture are rejected, we are left only with the authority of private opinion. If we go that route, the only possible destination will be ecclesiastical anarchy.

By reaffirming the biblical paradigm as the norm, at least some unity can be approached through careful and laborious exegesis. One thing is certain, neither party in the personal evangelism/social action dichotomy can appeal to the New Testament for support. That the New Testament commands both per-

160

sonal evangelism and social action is unequivocably clear to any sentient creature who takes the time to read it.

The Church as Holy

When the creed speaks of the church as holy and talks about a communion of saints, it is not introducing new extrabiblical categories of description. Rather, the idea of the church's being holy is firmly rooted in the Old and New Covenant community reality. In biblical categories, the covenant community is holy not so much in the sense that it is intrinsically righteous, but in the sense that it is separated, set apart, consecrated. The word "holy" has its roots in the Old Testament concept of division or separation from that which is profane. The word is pregnant in its content and carries a rich variety of nuances. However, the New Testament church is primarily "holy" in that it is set apart from profanity and exists in a unique relationship to Christ, who is the Holy One of Israel.

The New Testament word for church, *ekklesia*, carries a similar connotation. Literally, the term means "those called out." That is, those called by God to be in a peculiar relationship to Himself and to be involved in a vital task for God. Our English word "church" has been traced etymologically back through the Scottish word *kirk*, the Dutch *kerk*, the German *kirsche*, all the way back to the Greek *kuriache*, which means "those who belong to the Lord," the *kurios*.

The church is not only "holy" in the primary sense of being set apart but is "holy" in the sense of being clean or righteous. Here, the relationship or association with Christ is the basis of holiness, that is, the church is holy insofar as it is in union with Christ and is permeated by the presence and activity of the Holy Spirit.

Thus, the church is people, people called out of the theater of profanity to exist in union with Christ.

Hence, the New Testament speaks of the church in corporate and organic terms as the "body" of Christ, or the "people of God," or the "house of God," etc.

The Visible and Invisible Church

Much confusion exists concerning the meaning of the terms "visible" and "invisible" as adjectival descriptives of the church. The visible church refers to the church as an organization, as an institution. It numbers those people whose names appear "visibly" on the membership rolls of various churches. The invisible church does not refer to some phantom church or even to an underground movement outside of the visible church. Primarily, the term "invisible" has reference to those people within the visible church whose profession of faith is a genuine one. That is, those people who are truly "in Christ." The invisible church may include people whose names do not appear on the rolls of visible churches, but exists *substantially* within the visible church.

The conceptual distinction between visible/invisible church has its historical roots in the Donatist controversy of the fourth century, though the idea is clearly evident in the remnant concept of Israel in both Old and New Testaments. It was St. Augustine who defined the church as a *corpus permixtus*, i.e., a mixed body. The church contains tares along with wheat, unbelievers along with believers, those who worship with their lips while their hearts are far from Christ, as well as those who worship in Spirit and in truth. No man has the final authority or categorical ability to discern whose confession of faith is ultimately authentic. Hence, since the true Christian heart is not perceivable to us, but visible only to God, we speak of the invisible church. The degree of visibility of the holy people is a relative one and can vary from church to church and from age to age. The fruit of the Spirit need not be totally obscured, and it is our task to make the invisible church more visible through word and action.

When we seek the New Testament paradigm for the church, we are not seeking something merely invisible. The issue of the "true" church is not limited to invisibility, but has everything to do with the visible community. How can we define the true church? Where can we find it? This question has prompted various answers in history. Some have argued that where the Bishop is, there is the church. While others have argued that where the Spirit is, there is the church, still others have maintained that where the Word is truly preached and the sacraments properly administered, there is the church. More recently it has been argued that since the church has a "Pilgrim" character, it must be found in terms of its location and proximity to where "the action is," where God is working in our time. None of these succinct answers to the question seems to be adequate. One stresses government, another piety, another theology and sacramental perfection, and another social relevance. It seems the New Testament call that sanctifies the people of God includes all of these elements.

There is no perfect visible church. The New Testament church itself was not perfect and was frequently subject to apostolic rebuke and admonishment. However, we can gain directives from the New Testament as to what a church should be.

That New Testament churches had visible order and government is clearly evident from the texts. The "body" image was one that suggested the church was more than a spiritual organism that functioned chaotically. The Spirit is the spirit of order. What the proper ecclesiastical polity was is still a matter of great exegetical controversy, but that ecclesiastical government existed cannot be soberly disputed.

That the New Testament is concerned with piety and visible fruit of the Spirit is also evident. The people of God were clearly called to be transformed people,

people who were nonconformists to the profane world. This concept of moral and spiritual nonconformity was not restricted to the Old Testament, but was even more emphatic in the New Covenant. The degree of nonconformity has been a major problem and question to the historical church. The issue was raised in the monastic movement, the Separatist movement, and what we may call the modern "relevance" movement. The answer to the degree of nonconformity obligatory to the church is far beyond the scope of this book. That we are called to relate to the world is clear. That we are called to be righteous people is clear. That we are called to be distinctive people is clear. What that means in individual issues is not always clear. That the New Testament was not concerned with correct theology can only be argued by the most radical obscurantist. The content of God's Word was surely a matter of grave concern for the apostle Paul. As soon as we say, "I believe," we are talking theology, whether we like it or not. The Christian is inescapably involved in theology. To be a Christian is to be a theologian in one sense. We may be bad theologians, but theologians we must be. The contemporary disdain for correct theology was not shared by the apostolic church.

That the church is involved in a pilgrimage is also clear from the New Testament. That we should be participating in the redemptive activity of God in the world is a truism. Where God is acting in the world right now, however, is not always easy to discern. Often the answer to this question is given from the perspective of radical subjectivism or from the viewpoint of vested interests.

The history of the Christian church is, in many ways, the history of heresy and extremism, and the two are not unrelated. Heresy begets heresy, and extremism seems to be its mother. When the church errs, so often the corrective becomes extreme in the other direction. We seem to be in a period today of this kind of reaction. Where the past saw the existence of totalitarian and autocratic forms of church government, the present sees an underground movement against all ecclesiastical order and government. We replace one unbiblical model with another. Where the past saw severe discipline and punitive measures given to unrepentant members of churches involved in gross sin, and where big red A's were sewn to the blouses of adulterers, the church today gives virtually no reprimand, exercises virtually no discipline over its members. From severity of discipline to radical indulgence, the church swings from one extreme to the other.

Heresy trials in this day and age? Unthinkable! Where heretics formerly were burned and boiled, today they are not only tolerated but applauded for their candor of unbelief. From tightly bound confessional formulas, we have moved to theological relativism, subjectivism, and pluralism. The cliché remains, "The church that believes everything, believes nothing." Again, extremism is the order of the day.

Where once people like Simon Stylites sat on pillars and flagpoles to manifest nonconformity to the world, the present churchman often leaves his hermit's cave to embrace this world with so much fervor we frequently can't tell the difference between contemporary American culture and Christianity.

The questions we are dealing with are serious ones, and if we must be extreme, let us be extremely complex, rather than extremely simplistic. Simplistic answers will not do because they are *not* doing!

For this writer the future of the visible church appears to be a grim one, but not one that allows for total despair. Fresh winds seem to be blowing. A new concern for renovation and renewal in looking to the New Testament is evident. Perhaps the greatest hope for the future lies in the present revolution of the laity. A new dimension of lay involvement, lay education, and lay mobilization is informing the major churches of

Chapter 13

The Forgiveness of Sins;
the Resurrection of the Body;
and the Life Everlasting

With the confession of the forgiveness of sins, the creed
moves from the exposition of substantive theology to
the level of personal relationships. Perhaps the affirmation, "I believe in the forgiveness of sins," may be called
the quintessence of the Christian faith. At the expe-
riential or existential level of life, this means everything.

Forgiveness and Guilt

The word "forgiveness" presupposes the reality of
guilt. Forgiveness is meaningless if there is nothing to
be forgiven. Thus, to understand the full significance
of forgiveness, we must first understand the meaning
of guilt. Guilt is a multifaceted concept that is open to
all kinds of misunderstanding or variant interpretations. Primarily, the term has a legal connotation. That
is, it has reference to acts, or thoughts, etc., which
transgress a particular boundary established by law.
This law may vary from an abstract ethical principle to
a concrete piece of positivistic legislation. If an ethical
norm is violated or a standard transgressed, then guilt
is incurred.

In the juridical process of American society, a person is judged guilty or innocent of a particular charge of
failing to bring his behavior into conformity to the prescribed law. Thus, guilt is inseparably related to law.

167

Laws and Human Relationship

When a person is involved with law, he is also inevitably involved in human relationships. If a man commits a crime violating an ordinance or statute of a particular society, he is guilty not only of violating a principle, but also of violating the persons behind the principle. Where there is moral law, there is also a lawgiver or lawgivers. When a person is tried for a crime in a civil court, the charge is brought by the prosecutor with the preface of, "The State of Massachusetts, etc., against John Doe." In this framework, guilt involves a violation of the corporate body politic.

Guilt, of course, is not restricted to matters of civil or societal disobedience but can be incurred in a multitude of relationships between groups, private individuals, and indeed, even in relationship to one's self. A person may be "guilty" of violating his own private person. Nor can guilt be restricted to transgression of explicitly prescribed pieces of legislation or codified laws. Behavior may violate "unwritten" laws and incur guilt on the individual. Thus, guilt involves the wider question of human relationships.

Ultimately, guilt involves a relationship to God. In Him is the ultimate standard and the ultimate tribunal. The relationship involved is the covenant relationship of creature-Creator. Man as man is inescapably involved in a relationship to God. A person may despise that relationship or even deny the fact that it exists, but he cannot destroy it. The relationship may be a negative one, i.e., a relationship of severe alienation or estrangement, yet it remains a relationship.

The relationship that exists between God and man is not a neutral one. It is a relationship that involves moral obligation and responsibility. Man's privileged status in creation carries with it an enormous burden of moral responsibility both to God, to other men, to the self, and to the rest of the cosmos. (Here, then, is evidence that included in man's relationships is a relationship to the world of nature where matters of ecology, etc., become moral issues not merely because man does violence to himself by polluting his environment, but he also violates animals, plants, and other elements of the created order.) However, all secondary relationships with which we are involved are incorporated under the sovereign sphere of our relationship to God. We are responsible to God for our behavior toward other men, the cosmos, etc. In a word, man exists within the framework of *theonomy,* divine law.

Theonomy vs. Autonomy

Twentieth-century man is constantly involved in the question of freedom. The word is an emotive one over which murders have been committed and wars have been fought. Frequently the term "freedom" has been confused with the word "autonomy." "Autonomy" means literally "self-law." That is, a person who has autonomy is a law-unto-himself and is responsible to no one else for his behavior. Autonomy then is a particular kind of freedom, a freedom that involves not only the absence of restraint, but also the absence of responsibility to anyone but the self. This kind of "freedom" may be seen in Nietzsche's concept of "Master morality" and in Sartre's view of existential autonomy. This kind of "freedom," however, is not only immoral, but impossible for man to achieve. Society cannot and will not permit this view to prevail. Indeed, society is impossible in such terms. This is freedom in the context of moral and social anarchy, and reduces ethics to the level of the absurd.

That man desires autonomy is not difficult to manifest. That he has it is quite another matter. In fact, man does not live in the context of autonomy, but in the context of theonomy, i.e., under the law of God. The conflict between the desire for self-law and the obligation to submit to the law of God is at the root of the human predicament. The primordial temptation that provokes the fall of Adam and Eve is the serpentine suggestion, "You shall be as God. . . ." This narrative indicates that inseparable from the fall of man is his desire for autonomy and his reluctance to exist under the government of God.

Herein is the foundation of all human guilt that rests in a real spirit and act of disobedience to the command of God. This, the Scriptures call "sin." This is what makes forgiveness necessary for us to experience authentic manhood. The word "sin" is an unpleasant term and carries with it all sorts of ghastly connotations. However unpleasant it is, it is nevertheless real and devastating in its destructive capability. Sin is evil, not merely because it involves the violation of rules, but because it involves the violation of persons. When I sin against another person, I injure that person, I damage myself, and I bring dishonor and disgrace to God, whose image we both bear. We can describe "sin" in terms of "finitude," "inauthentic existence," or "psychological neurosis," but none of these terms mitigate in the slightest the radical seriousness of the injury that is effected by sin.

Biblically, the term "sin" means literally "to miss the mark." The mark that is missed is the standard God imposes on man for His righteousness. Theonomy means not only that God operates as judge, but it means that He sets the standard for judgment. It is not within man's province to dictate his own ethical norm. Rather, he receives it from God and is responsible to it.

There is much confusion concerning the meaning of the terms "good" and "bad," particularly in the moral sphere. These words are relative words. That is, their concrete meaning cannot be known in themselves, but only as they relate to standards. Something may be said to be good or bad compared to the standard established of goodness and/or badness. Biblically, the standard ultimately is given by God and is not a matter of human legislation. When we fail to meet the divine

170

standard of righteousness, then we are involved with *guilt.*

Guilt and the Feeling of Guilt

It is important that the Christian as well as the non-believer understands the critical difference between guilt and guilt feelings. Guilt refers to something objective, that is, to a status quite independent of one's feelings. The feeling of guilt refers to something subjective, something that goes on within the emotive make-up of the person involved. The feeling of guilt may or may not accurately correspond to the reality of the situation. That is, a person may be guilty of something and not "feel" guilty about it. Conversely, a person may "feel" guilty, but not be actually guilty of any crime. Human beings must distinguish between the two as we are all involved with both feelings of guilt and real guilt. It is crucially important that we are able to recognize when our feelings of guilt are rooted in real or imaginary guilt. This becomes a critical practical problem to the counselor or psychiatrist who must deal with people's feelings. If the feelings are rooted in real guilt, then dealing only with the feeling-level of symptoms may cause irreparable damage. There is a distinct difference between rationalization and forgiveness. The former seeks to deny the guilt while the latter seeks to heal it. To confuse the two is the worst kind of Christian Science, which seeks to dispel the warning signals of real sickness by arguing that pain is unreal. Thus, the pastoral counselor or psychiatrist is often unavoidably caught in making ethical judgments that have far-reaching import.

Guilt and Conscience

There is a popular aphorism that says, "Let your conscience be your guide." This slogan, of course, has more to do with Jiminy Cricket than with the New Testament. In no sense does the New Testament regard the conscience as the highest tribunal of man's ethical behavior. This would involve a subtle form of subjectivistic autonomy. The conscience may accuse or excuse us at the feeling level of existence, but cannot be the ultimate standard of righteousness. We are aware of the common phenomenon of a person's desensitizing his conscience through repeated acts of crime to the point where he can commit gross and heinous deeds with no feeling of remorse. On the other side of the coin, there is the unfortunate person who has been brainwashed into thinking certain things are wrong which in fact are not wrong. Here, the conscience can be distorted in the other direction of hypersensitivity.

The desensitized conscience as well as the hypersensitive conscience are dangerous distortions to man's ethical well-being. Both can be inseparably related to the compounding of real guilt. The former causes the sinner to be at ease in his crime, removing the bars of self-restraint, and producing a greater yield of sin. The latter is a more complicated matter. If a person thinks that a particular act is evil (when, in fact, in and of itself it is ethically neutral), and proceeds to commit that act, then the person is guilty of sin, namely, the sin of doing something he thought to be evil. For example, if a person is raised in an environment that teaches emphatically that playing bridge is a sin (when it obviously is not) and comes to believe that bridge playing is sinful, then proceeds to play bridge, he is then guilty of sin. The guilt is located not in the bridge playing *per se,* but rather in the act of going against his conscience, deliberately doing something he judged to be evil.

Though the New Testament does not regard the conscience as the ultimate test of righteousness, it does not consider the conscience unimportant. But since the conscience is capable of corruption and distortion, the Christian is exhorted to seek the sanctification of his conscience. The carnal mind must be transformed by the Holy Spirit and conformed to the Word of God if it is to be a suitable guide for ethical behavior.

Conviction and Accusation of Sin

The Christian ethic is manifestly supernatural in many ways. It is an ethic that transcends the earthly sphere in that the basis for it is in God. God does not restrict Himself to being lawgiver, but He also enters our situation in the person of the Holy Spirit in convicting us of our sin. That is, God deals with the consciences of men. He can and does often incite our moral sense and quickens us with a feeling of guilt. However, as already mentioned, God is not the only stimulator of the conscience, and special care is needed to discern the difference between the conviction of the Holy Spirit and other kinds of conviction.

This difficulty is compounded by the reality of the demonic sphere of influence. The reality of satanic activity in ethical situations should not be underestimated. Traditionally, satanic activity in the life of the Christian has usually been associated with temptation. Indeed, the Evil One does manifest himself as the tempter. However, his activity is not limited to temptation. One of the most devastating influences wrought on the Christian by the devil is his work of accusation. In this capacity, the enemy seeks to undermine the peace of the Christian that is the fruit of forgiveness. He seeks to make present, past guilt that has been forgiven and forgotten by God. He seeks to destroy the confidence that is the fruit of justification. He seeks to convince the Christian that he must atone for his own sins. This power of accusation cannot be minimized as it strikes at the very heart of the Christian's faith. Satan troubles the conscience that has already been at rest in Christ.

How can a man tell the difference between the conviction of God the Holy Spirit and the accusation of

Satan? This discernment is not always easy. Its difficulty is increased by the fact that Satan has metamorphic powers. That is, he is able to transform himself into one having the appearance of an angel of light, seeking to confuse us in the masquerade. The discernment, however, must be made if the Christian is to have an abiding peace. When the Spirit convicts a believer of sin He does not drive him to despair. The Spirit may trouble, upset, or distress the Christian, but His convicting power does not destroy what Christ has redeemed. On the other hand, the accusation of Satan is brutal, seeking to paralyze the Christian in the bondage of servile fear. It is against such vicious attack that Paul can cry out: "Who will bring a charge against God's elect? God is the one who justifies . . ." (Rom. 8:33). In a sense Paul is saying: "Sticks and stones . . . Satan . . . get off my back!" Paul's confidence rested in the merit of Christ and in God's promise of forgiveness.

A word of caution needs to be given at this point. Though there does seem to be a discernible difference in the feeling pattern associated with conviction of sin by the Holy Spirit and the accusation of Satan, we dare not rest our case with this kind of discernment. It is not enough to establish some kind of calculus of feeling-associations as they can often be deceptive. The only sure test for discerning the difference between the conviction of the Holy Spirit and that of Satan is the test of Scripture. In the Word of God we can learn enough about God and enough about Satan, enough about real guilt and enough about real forgiveness to give us adequate ability to make the necessary differentiation.

Forgiveness and the Feeling of Forgiveness

As a distinction has already been made between the *reality* of guilt and *feeling* of guilt, so also must a similar distinction be made between the reality of forgiveness and the feeling of forgiveness. This is made imperative by the fact that so many contemporary Christians are basically *sensual* in their faith. That is, they seem to ride the tide of rising and falling feeling levels. This is not to imply that the Christian ought to be devoid of feeling. On the contrary, ours is a most passionate faith. But the truth of Christ rests on reality, not on our feelings about it.

This issue of reality and feeling is particularly important when we speak about forgiveness. Again, there is an objective-subjective distinction. Real forgiveness between God and man rests on the declaration of God. When God declares a person forgiven, that person is forgiven whether he feels it or not. Again we appeal to the analogy of the courtroom situation. If a man is convicted of a crime and the judge decides to show mercy and grant a pardon, removing the penalty for the crime, the defendant is in fact pardoned. He may not feel pardoned; he may still feel guilty (which indeed he is); he may feel that he wants to pay for his crime, yet none of these feelings changes the objective state of affairs, namely, that the man has been pardoned.

The basis of the Christian's assurance of forgiveness is the promise of God. The New Testament tells us unequivocally, "If we confess our sins, He is faithful and righteous to forgive us our sins and to cleanse us from all unrighteousness" (1 John 1:9). John's statement, of course, is only one among many. Repeatedly we are given the assurance in the New Testament that our God is a forgiving God. Part of the content of faith in the New Testament sense is that element that includes confidence in the promise of God. That is, my assurance of forgiveness should be based on my confidence that God means what He says and does what He says He will do. If God declares that He will forgive our sins if we ask for that forgiveness in the spirit of confession, then we can have confidence that those sins we have confessed are forgiven in fact.

The feeling of forgiveness may or may not follow the

reality. It is difficult to get justification by faith into our bloodstream. We may understand the doctrine intellectually and apprehend something of the meaning of the cross quite readily, but to feel it is often difficult. Indeed, the forgiveness that comes to us in Christ is an astonishing thing. It is hard for us to feel the full force of the fact that the penalty for our sin has already been paid and that the judgment on us has already been executed on Christ. That the work of atonement is finished staggers our minds. Daily we must remind ourselves that there is *nothing*, absolutely nothing of merit, that we can add to the Atonement of Christ, or subtract from it. If indeed we possess the righteousness of Christ, how much more do we need? Again, our forgiveness rests not on our feelings, but on the work of Christ.

Though the distinction between forgiveness and the feeling of forgiveness must be made, this is not to suggest in the slightest that the Christian cannot and does not experience both. There is nothing more blessed than to be forgiven and to feel the peace that attends the reality. We do have peace with God and a glorious peace it is. Forgiveness by God is something to get excited about. To experience the influence of grace on the heart is to know joy unspeakable. Real forgiveness for real guilt is what stimulates the Christian to songs of praise, thanksgiving, and adoration. One of the primary inducements to godliness and good works is not that we might atone for our past sins, but that we may demonstrate with clarity the depth of our gratitude to our merciful Father. Jesus indicated this kind of a response when He said, "Which of them therefore will love him more? . . . The one whom he forgave more" (Luke 7:42–43). This ratio of proportionate forgiveness/love may induce the Christian to seek a deeper understanding of the extent to which God has been gracious to us.

Again, a distinction must be made between a feeling

of forgiveness and a feeling of innocence. The two are not the same. Our general dispositions may be similar with regard to the peace of innocence and the peace of forgiveness. But forgiveness does not mean we are declared innocent by God. We receive the treatment and the payment of the innocent, but that should not lead us to believe that we are innocent. Again, real forgiveness presupposes real guilt. Innocence cannot be forgiven.

Forgiveness and Repentance

Forgiveness is not granted automatically to the world via the cross. Prerequisites are demanded by God. We must take seriously the biblical call to repentance. That call comes to us not as an invitation, but as a command. Paul states it clearly: "God is now declaring to men that all everywhere should repent" (Acts 17:30b). Here, repentance is not optional, but obligatory. Repentance is the *sine qua non* of forgiveness.

Repentance is an important New Testament word, and again, one that carries various shades of meaning. Literally, the term means "change of mind." It involves looking at things and values, etc., from a new perspective. It includes viewing our sin as it really is, without rationalization. It includes repudiating the sin in our lives, and involves in its depth, a spirit of contrition.

Contrition and Attrition

Historically, there has been considerable debate on the matter of the relationship between attrition and contrition to forgiveness.[1] Simply stated, attrition is that kind of "repentance" that is motivated primarily by a fear of punishment. That is, clinging to the mercy of God as a ticket out of hell, or an escape route from His punitive wrath.

---

[1]This issue is particularly relevant to the Reformation dispute concerning the Roman Catholic sacrament of penance. Discussion of this matter would necessitate an extensive theological treatment, which is beyond the scope of this book.

Contrition, on the other hand, goes beyond the scope of attrition to a sense of genuine sorrow for having offended God by our sin. It is contrition that the New Testament calls us to in order to receive the forgiveness of God. The spirit of genuine contrition may be best illustrated by Psalm 51. Here, David cries:

> Wash me thoroughly from my iniquity, and cleanse me from my sin. For I know my transgressions, and my sin is ever before me. Against Thee, Thee only, I have sinned, and done what is evil in Thy sight, so that Thou art justified when Thou dost speak, and blameless when Thou dost judge (vv. 2–4).

Here, the confession is pointed. There is no attempt by the psalmist to declare his innocence, to minimize his guilt, or to deprive God of His right to judge him. He concludes with the following declaration:

> For Thou dost not delight in sacrifice, otherwise I would give it; Thou art not pleased with burnt offering. The sacrifices of God are a broken spirit; a broken and a contrite heart, O God, Thou wilt not despise (vv. 16–17).

Indeed, God does not despise brokenness and contrition. His response to these postures of penitence is a response of forgiveness.

Cheap Grace

It was Bonhoeffer who wrote extensively on the subject of "cheap grace." So often forgiveness is conceived in maudlin terms. Other times it is assured as something God automatically confers on everyone, with or without repentance. Such a view of forgiveness involves a serious distortion of the New Testament. It is worse than presumption to assume the forgiveness of God when no repentance has taken place. It makes grace not only cheap, but worthless. An "automatic" view of grace takes the graciousness out of grace. That is to say that grace is robbed of its essence, the voluntary extension of mercy to those who repent.

To proclaim the gospel, the good news of forgiveness is at the core of the church's commission. Indeed, the announcement of forgiveness is good news to those who know the reality of guilt. However, zeal to communicate the goodness of God must never obscure the sober call of the New Testament to earnest and honest repentance.

Liberation and Salvation

In contemporary theology there is a movement that threatens to obscure the meaning of Christian salvation and forgiveness. Liberation theology, particularly as seen in Latin America, struggles with many important social issues. Yet it tends to reduce salvation to the struggle for socio-economic liberation.

Representatives of liberation theology include Roman Catholics such as Assmann, Segundo, and Gutierrez, and Protestants such as Alvez, Castro, and Bonino. Their theology begins in an understanding of social problems. Gutierrez defines the purpose of liberation theology in his work *A Theology of Liberation*.

"It is a theological reflection born of the experience of shared efforts to abolish the current unjust situations and to build a different society, freer and more human."[2]

Gutierrez sees theology as a reflection on the historical "praxis," the everyday social political reality of living. As the historical praxis changes so does theology. Thus terms like "salvation," "kingdom of God," and "faith" change along with the historical situation. As critical reflection on society changes, theology changes. "In the last analysis the true interpretation of the meaning revealed by theology is achieved only in

---

[2]Gustavo Gutierrez, *A Theology of Liberation* (Maryknoll, N. Y.: Orbis Books, 1973), p. IX.

historical praxis. . . . We have here a political hermeneutics of the Gospel."[3]

In Gutierrez' thought, theology tends to become a symbolic way of talking about society. Salvation is no longer directly related to sin, faith, and justification but becomes political liberation. Clark Pinnock says:

> You often can get the distinct impression that political analysis has taken precedence over biblical theology. Gutierrez, for example, gets halfway through his book before engaging any scriptural concepts, and his book is in many ways the textbook of the movement. Then when he does discuss biblical ideas, his selection of themes like exodus and liberation and his omission of themes like justification and sin lead the reader to suspect that Scripture is being used to sustain positions developed outside its orbit.[4]

Gutierrez begins with the universalistic assumption that all people now participate in Christ and then concentrates exclusively on the historical form salvation takes—building new society.

Harvie Conn points out: "Salvation is transformed into economic, political liberation, Christology into love of our neighbor, eschatology into politics, church into humanity, sacraments into human solidarity."[5]

The danger of Latin American liberation theology and other similar movements is that there is a claim to a Christian view of salvation without proclaiming man's need to be saved from sin through faith in Christ.

---

[3]Ibid., pp. 12–13; see also p. 54.

[4]Clark Pinnock, "Liberation Theology: The Gains, The Gaps," *Christianity Today,* (January 16, 1976): 14.

[5]Harvie M. Conn, "The Mission of the Church" in *Evangelicals and Liberation,* ed. Carl Armerding (Nutley, N.J.: 1977), p. 82.

The Resurrection of the Body
and the Life Everlasting

Whatever else man is, he is a creature with a physical nature. We may be lyrical in our praise for the spiritual dimension of man, we may exalt the intellectual capacities he enjoys, we may delight in the uniqueness of the soul, but none of these aspects of human existence negates the stark reality of man's physical life.

The phenomenologist has wisely pointed out that man's body is the point of contact or transition between the self and the world. The Marxist has seen that man's bodily life in terms of his labor and his economics has much to do with his history. The psychiatrist knows the intimate relationship that exists between body and mind. The physician knows that sickness and pain are realities that greatly affect the status and the well-being of the self. The athlete knows the pleasure involved in bodily exercise. The married person understands the significance of sex to human communication and love. In thousands of ways, man's flesh contributes to his being a man.

As I write these lines, I am very much aware of the many ways in which the state of the body affects the self. This is the last chapter of my book and I am eager to complete it. This day has been set apart for writing. Yet, at this moment I am torn between writing and going to bed. My mind is muddled as antibiotics are racing through my bloodstream on a search-and-destroy mission against the enemy of my present well-being, a sinus infection. My wife has been sick for three weeks, and as a result I have found myself given to irritability. None of these maladies is serious. They are but minor inconveniences and petty annoyances that attend the daily life of every person. But even these affect in a very real way the process we call living. We are living in the context of bodies. But bodies die, . . . there is inevitable decay and disintegration that awaits the body of every man. The body is conceived, it is born, it experiences

181

growth and undergoes changes, it ages and moves all too rapidly toward the experience of death.

To call death the "last and greatest enemy" of man is not to use unwarranted hyperbole. That we die is no small thing. The existentialist has said much about what the reality of death means to our existence. Volumes have appeared dealing with the anxiety that is common to the man who contemplates the threat of non-being. Our funeral practices betray our inability to face the realities of death. Death evokes fear and we seem trapped in the midst of an inevitable and insoluble dilemma.

It is to this precise dilemma that the Christian faith speaks with clarity and with significance. There is no maudlin view of immortality in the sense that our "memories" live on and we continue beyond the grave in the remembrance of our loved ones. That is no more consolation to us than an elaborate funeral or magnificent tomb. What we want is life, not monuments. Nor does the New Testament attempt to console man in his predicament by appealing to speculative analogies in nature as the basis for hope in life beyond the grave. Because the caterpillar undergoes a metamorphosis on his way to becoming a butterfly is no guarantee that our final destiny will be any better than that of the butterfly when it dies. Nor is the Christian at the mercy of the wizard or necromancer to gain insight into life after death. The Christian looks not to speculation or to magic for his hope, rather, he looks to history.

The most astonishing message proclaimed by the apostles was the declaration that Jesus of Nazareth arose from the dead. This resurrection was not seen as an isolated event, extraordinary as it was, but carried with it the promise that we shall also participate in the power of resurrection. It is in the event of the Resurrection and in the subsequent promise of the resurrected One that the church bases her hope in victory over death.

Resurrection and Immortality

Much confusion often arises between the Christian concept of resurrection and the Greek view of immortality (most notably articulated by Plato). The two are not synonymous. To be sure, there are parallels between them. Both views affirm that there is continuity of life beyond the grave. But the differences are great and quite important.

The Greek view of immortality rests its hope for eternal life on its view of the indestructible and eternal character of the soul. The soul will continue to live because it always has lived. It existed prior to birth and will continue after the body decays. The soul itself is intrinsically eternal. It is nonmaterial and is incapable of annihilation. It may return to the earth in another receptacle, but it will not, indeed, it cannot die. To the Greek, the body is the prison house of the soul and not until the soul is released from its captor is redemption accomplished.

Quite to the contrary, the biblical doctrine of man contains no such pagan concept of immortality of the soul. The soul is created at conception.[6] It has no intrinsic self-existence apart from the creative and sustaining power of God. While the Bible teaches that the soul survives death in an intermediate form of existence, this does not exhaust the Christian hope of eternal life.[7] Also of critical importance is the fact that, biblically, redemption includes the body. Where the Greek sees redemption as being from the body, the New Testament sees redemption as being *of* the body. Thus,

---

[6]The biblical word "soul" is attended with a variety of nuances of meaning. It has been frequently understood in Greek categories that do little to clarify biblical understanding. A detailed analysis of "soul" is beyond the scope of this book. See J. A. Schep, *The Nature of the Resurrection Body* (Grand Rapids: Eerdmans, 1964), for a more extensive study of this question.

[7]Luke 23:43; 2 Corinthians 5:8; Philippians 1:23; Westminster Confession XXXII, par. 1.

the Christian looks forward not simply to an extended life of the soul, but also to a resurrected body.

The nature of our resurrected body is a subject of much dispute. That the resurrected body will be identical to the present body does not seem to be the case. However, there is room for assuming there will be some abiding similarity. The usual clue to answering this thorny question is found in relation to the postresurrection body of Jesus. The problem is complicated, however, by the fact that the nature of His resurrected body is not entirely clear to us. We know He was seen of men, that He ate and conversed with His friends. There is the suggestion that He possibly walked through closed doors in the Upper Room (though the text doesn't say that explicitly). Jesus gives the invitation to Thomas to touch the wounds in His body, though the record never states whether Thomas did, in fact, touch them. Questions arise out of the apparent inability of Mary to recognize the risen Christ immediately in the garden. Her confusion of Jesus with the gardener raises questions. Was the confusion due to Mary's emotional distress or was it due to a substantial change in the appearance of Christ's body? The same issue is raised in the failure of the men on the road to Emmaus to recognize Jesus as they walked with Him and even discussed the circumstances of His death. The answers to these questions remain cloaked somewhat in mystery. What we can be sure of is that whatever the resurrected body of Jesus was and is like, it is the paradigm for our own resurrected state. John writes:

> Beloved, now we are children of God, and it has not appeared as yet what we shall be. We know that, when He appears, we shall be like Him, because we shall see Him just as He is (1 John 3:2).

The New Testament carries a certain amount of self-confessed mystery of these matters. Indeed, we are not left in total ignorance but we "see through a glass dimly." The apostle Paul sheds some light on the question when he instructs the Corinthians regarding the resurrection: "Just as we have borne the image of the earthy, we shall also bear the image of the heavenly" (1 Cor. 15:49).

Earlier, the apostle argues that even on the earthly plane of existence there are various kinds of flesh among the animals, and speaks of variant kinds of bodies, celestial and terrestrial. He concludes:

> So also is the resurrection of the dead. It is sown a perishable *body*, it is raised an imperishable *body*; it is sown in dishonor, it is raised in glory; it is sown in weakness, it is raised in power; it is sown a natural body, it is raised a spiritual body. If there is a natural body, there is also a spiritual *body* (1 Cor. 15:42–44).

Here, the resurrected body of man is contrasted with the present body in terms of four pairs of contrasts: perishable/imperishable, dishonor/glory, weakness/power, and physical/spiritual.

It is the last distinction that causes the most perplexity. What in the world is a "spiritual body"? This statement must cause us some consternation as we are accustomed to think of spirit and body in terms of polar opposites. Perhaps this passage should serve to warn us against reading into the Hebrew categories of spiritual and physical those categories that we use today. We like to think in terms of material and immaterial, extension and nonextension, or even matter and energy. Obviously, Paul is not thinking like that. In the context of the passage he is speaking of a real body that is in some way analogous to other earthly bodies, yet a body that is qualitatively and ontologically different. The precise nature, however, of a "spiritual body" remains an enigma to us. This enigma is not strange in that Paul is describing a future bodily state that is not accessible to our empirical scrutiny and analysis at the present time. But the promise remains that God will clothe His people with a new kind of body, one that is superior to the present, and that we will not abide forever in the state of nakedness as disembodied spirits.

The Spirit-Flesh Dichotomy

At many points in the writing of Paul, it seems as though he has been heavily influenced by the Greek dichotomy between spirit and flesh. He discusses the experience of the Christian life in terms of a warfare between the spirit and the flesh. This is often misunderstood as meaning a negation of the physical life of man.

Part of this misunderstanding can be eliminated if we understand the New Testament usage of the term "body" or "flesh." The Greek has two different words, both capable of being rendered in English by the word "body." The first is *soma*. The term *soma* has been incorporated into the English language and is used frequently in the word psychosomatic. *Soma* refers to the physical or bodily aspects of man. (A psychosomatic illness is one that is caused by psychic disturbances that manifest themselves in real somatic or bodily symptoms.)

The meaning of *soma* is not too difficult to discern. However, the meaning of its sister term, *sarx*, is more troublesome. This term can also be translated by the word "body" or "flesh," but does not always have specific reference to the bodily dimension of man's life. Particularly when Paul sets the term "spirit" *(pneuma)* in opposition to "flesh" *(sarx)*, we see him using the term figuratively. Here, Paul describes a warfare between two qualitatively different life styles. The life style of the godly man, or the new dimension of regenerate man informed by the Holy Spirit is contrasted with that life style manifested in natural and carnal man. This is not warfare between mind and body or between the spiritual and physical. Carnality or "fleshiness" in this context is a description of a negative quality of life. Here, the mind and the soul, the physical and the spiritual aspect of man is described as corrupt.

The Scriptures do not allow an intrinsically negative value to be attached to physical things. God created a physical world and gave it His benediction, calling it good. The promises of both New and Old Covenants include physical blessing. Failure to understand this has caused the church to distort the message of the gospel all too frequently in the history of Christianity. Because of the influx of Platonic ideas, the church has often demeaned the value of the physical and we are left with too negative a view of creation, negating the world, the physical needs of man, sex, and many other beautiful and good aspects of the created order. The physical was created by God and it will be redeemed by God as we look not to the destruction of the heaven and the earth, but for renovation—to a new heaven and a new earth where God's creation will be redeemed, not obliterated.

Bibliography

Barth, Karl. *Church Dogmatics,* Vol. IV/1. Edinburgh: T. & T. Clark, 1956.

Berkhouwer, G. C. *The Person of Christ.* Grand Rapids: Eerdmans, 1952.

_____. *The Work of Christ.* Grand Rapids: Eerdmans, 1952.

Bruce, F. F. *The New Testament Development of Old Testament Themes.* Grand Rapids: Eerdmans, 1968.

Brunner, Emil. *The Christian Doctrine of God.* Philadelphia: Westminster, 1950.

_____. *The Christian Doctrine of the Church, Faith, and the Consummation.* Philadelphia: Westminster, 1962.

_____. *The Mediator.* Philadelphia: Westminster, 1957.

_____. *Revelation and Reason.* Philadelphia: Westminster, 1946.

Bultmann, Rudolf. *Jesus Christ and Mythology.* New York: Scribner, 1958.

_____. *Kerygma and Myth.* ed. H. W. Bartsch. New York: Harper & Row, 1961.

Carnell, E. J. *An Introduction to Christian Apologetics.* Grand Rapids: Eerdmans, 1948.

Casserley, J. V. L. *The Christian in Philosophy.* New York: Scribner, 1960.

Clark, Gordon. *A Christian View of Men and Things.* Grand Rapids: Eerdmans, 1952.

Cullmann, Oscar. *The Christology of the New Testament.* Philadelphia: Westminster, 1959.

_____. *Christ and Time.* Philadelphia: Westminster, 1964.

_____. *Salvation in History.* New York: Harper, 1967.

Edwards, Jonathan. *The Works of President Edwards.* Vol. III. New York: Carter, 1879.

Eichrodt, Walter. *Theology of the Old Testament.* Vol. II. Philadelphia: Westminster, 1961.

Farley, Edward. *The Transcendence of God.* Philadelphia: Westminster, 1958.

Ferré, Frederick. *Language, Logic, and God.* New York: Harper, 1961.

Geldenhuys, J. N. *Commentary on the Gospel of Luke* Grand Rapids: Eerdmans, 1951.

Gollwitzer, Helmut. *The Existence of God as Confessed by Faith.* Philadelphia: Westminster, 1965.

Hick, John. *Faith and Knowledge.* Ithaca: Cornell University Press, 1957.

Jacob, Edmond. *Theology of the Old Testament.* New York: Harper, 1958.

Kittel, G. (ed.) *Theological Dictionary of the New Testament.* Vol. I. Grand Rapids: Eerdmans, 1964.

Kline, Meredith. *By Oath Consigned.* Grand Rapids: Eerdmans, 1968.

_____. *Treaty of the Great King.* Grand Rapids: Eerdmans, 1963.

Küng, Hans. *Justification,* New York: Nelson, 1964.

Kuyper, Abraham. *The Work of the Holy Spirit.* Grand Rapids: Eerdmans, 1956.

Luther, Martin. *Bondage of the Will.* Westwood, N.J.: Revell, 1957.

Melville, Herman. *Moby Dick.* ed. Alfred Kazin. Cambridge, Mass.: Riverside Press, 1956.

Mendenhall, George. *Law and Covenant in Israel and the Ancient Near East.* Pittsburgh, Pa.: The Biblical Colloquium, 1955.

Montgomery, John W. *History and Christianity.* Downers Grove, Ill.: Inter-Varsity Press, 1964.

Murray, John. *Principles of Conduct.* Grand Rapids: Eerdmans, 1957.

Pinnock, Clark. *Biblical Revelation.* Chicago: Moody Press, 1971.

Richardson, Herbert. *Toward an American Theology.* New York: Harper, 1967.

Robinson, James M. *A New Quest of the Historical Jesus.* London: SCM, 1959.

Schep, J. A. *The Nature of the Resurrection Body.* Grand Rapids: Eerdmans, 1964.

Schweitzer, Albert. *The Quest of the Historical Jesus.* New York: Macmillan, 1961.

Van Buren, Paul M. *The Secular Meaning of the Gospel.* New York: Macmillan, 1963.

Vos, Geerhardus. *Biblical Theology.* Grand Rapids: Eerdmans, 1951.